Whom Seek

Fr Jonathan Munn OblOSB

Published by the Anglican Catholic Church – Diocese of the United Kingdom

© 2019 Fr Jonathan Munn OblOSB. All rights reserved.

IṢBN 978-0-244-15331-1

Foreword

By the Rt Rev Damien Mead
Bishop Ordinary - Diocese of the United Kingdom
Anglican Catholic Church

This book has been written to fulfil an important and urgent need for this Diocese in providing an opportunity for newcomers to the Anglican Catholic Church to explore what we believe and why. There is nothing new or unique in our Faith and Practice as traditional Anglican Catholics, we do not claim to be THE one true Church - but believe we are part of THE One True Church. Father Jonathan Munn, OblOSB, has risen to the challenge I gave him when commissioning this book and I thank him and heartily recommend it.

Everyone comes to the same Christian Faith from a different direction, and we believe that, while the Church's doctrine is fixed, our journey to and within that doctrine is not and needs careful guidance. There can be no one-size-fits-all approach to catechism (teaching the faith) especially in the present day and age in which self-discovery is high in the minds of people. There is, within the following pages, clear opportunity and direction for the newcomer to learn from discussion with a mentor. One simply cannot learn the faith by books: it must be lived with others. Even the reading of Holy Scripture needs to be read in a Christian community for it to inform and encourage the soul.

Readers can rest assured that, although the Anglican Catholic Church is very small in the United Kingdom, it has people within it who are happy to share their journeys to God with those who are interested. The practice of the Catholic Religion must come from the heart. This book seeks to help reconcile what we believe with what we do, and readers would do well to see how the Works of Mercy fit in with their lives. Our duty to tend to the needs of others must be informed by what we believe, and not the other way around as some may think in this day and age.

+Damien

Contents

Foreword 3
Chapter 1: Who am I? 10
    You 10
    Us 11
Chapter 2: Who is God? 14
    The Nicene Creed 14
    I believe 15
    I believe in one God, the Father Almighty 16
    Maker of Heaven and Earth, and of all things visible and invisible 18
    And in one Lord Jesus Christ, ... 19
    Who, for us men and for our salvation, ... 21
    And was crucified also for us under Pontius Pilate; He suffered and was buried; 23
    And the third day He rose again, according to the Scriptures; 25
    And ascended into heaven, ... 26
    And sitteth on the right hand of the Father; 27
    And I believe in the Holy Ghost, The Lord and Giver of Life; 28
    Who proceedeth from the Father [and the Son], ... 30
    Who spake by the prophets. 32
    And I believe one 33
    Holy 36
    Catholic 38
    And apostolic Church. 39

I acknowledge one baptism for the remission of sins; 41

And I look for the resurrection of the dead, ... 43

And the life of the world to come. Amen. 45

Chapter 3: How do I respond to God? 47

    Prayer, Fasting and Giving Alms. 47

    Keeping the Commandments. 49

    Repentance. 52

    Reading the Bible 55

    Good deeds. 57

    Committing to the Church and Living the Faith 58

Chapter 4: How do I talk with God? 61

    Prayer in general 61

    Our Father. 62

    Who art in Heaven 63

    Hallowed be Thy name. 64

    Thy Kingdom come 65

    Thy Will be done in Earth as it is in Heaven 66

    Give us this day our daily bread 67

    And forgive us our trespasses as we forgive those who trespass against us. 69

    And lead us not into temptation, but deliver us from Evil 71

    Amen 72

    The Intercession of the Saints. 73

    Praying for the Dead 75

Chapter 5: How do I know Good and Evil? 77

    Gluttony versus Abstinence and Temperance 78

    Avarice versus Generosity 79

    Lust versus Chastity and Continence 82

    Sloth versus Diligence 84

    Pride and Vanity versus Humility 85

    Wrath versus Patience 87

    Envy versus Kindness 89

    But Remember! 90

Chapter 6: What does the Church offer me? 93

    Grace 93

    Baptism 94

    The Mass 96

    Confirmation 99

    Confession 100

    Holy Matrimony 102

    Extreme Unction 103

    Holy Orders 105

Chapter 7: What does the world get wrong? 111

    Life after Death? 111

    Mary, Queen of Heaven 115

    Angels and Archangels 117

    The Devil 118

    Miracles 121

    Prayer books, Breviaries and Missals 123

The Blessed Sacrament	124
Ikons and Idols	125
The Church Year and its Seasons	126
Chapter 8: Who am I?	**131**
Your Prayer Life	131
Your Study	131
Your Work as a Christian	132
Your Relationship with God	132
Chapter 9: What is going to happen to me?	**133**
Reception	133
Baptism	133
Confirmation	134
And now?	134
Appendix	**136**
Selected Prayers to Learn and Use	136
Sign of the Cross	136
The Lord's Prayer	136
Hail Mary	136
Glory Be	136
Apostles' Creed	137
Come, Holy Ghost	137
Grace before meals	137
Salve Regina	137
Prayer to St Michael the Archangel	137

The Athanasian Creed 138
The Works of Mercy 140
   The Seven Corporal Works of Mercy 140
   The Seven Spiritual Works of Mercy 140
Index 141

Chapter 1: Who am I?

You

Let us begin with you. If you are reading this, then you are probably making a decision to be received into the Anglican Catholic Church, or Baptised or Confirmed as a Christian. You are thinking about this decision because it matters to you a great deal even if you can't always put your thoughts and feelings into words. There is a desire within you to come closer to God through our Lord Jesus Christ, and you are trying to see if we, the Anglican Catholic Church, can help you find God. Hopefully, you have a Mentor – a priest or experienced layperson – to help you work your way through your preparation. This Guide is designed to help you think through the central issues of what we believe, and help you develop your understanding so that you can begin a purposeful life in the Christian Faith. Please do the exercises that follow so that you can make the most of this preparation time, and come to enter the Church as a member of the Body of Christ.

Perhaps:

1) You have just become a Christian and want to be Baptised. (Some people might say "Christened") You need to find out more about what Baptism means.
2) You were Baptised as a baby and you now want to be Confirmed. Your Godparents made promises on your behalf, but now you need to know what you are going to be taking on from them.
3) You are being received into the Anglican Catholic Church from somewhere else. You need to know how we differ, and where you fit in.

In all three cases, this is about you and your relationship with the Church of Our Lord Jesus Christ. Know now that we are very excited about getting to know you as a member with us and look forward to helping you make your decision. Let us start with an exercise.

Exercise 1.1

Think about your expectations for what lies ahead in this preparation. Who do you understand God to be? How would you describe your relationship with Him right now? Discuss these with your Mentor.

Us

Before we examine what we believe and how we express it, we ought to say a little bit about ourselves so that you can understand where we're coming from and thus see how we approach the same questions that you're asking. Remember, these are very likely to be the same questions that many Christians have asked through the centuries.

We are the Anglican Catholic Church, and we believe ourselves to be inheritors of the Catholic Faith as received historically through the Church in England.

We're not Roman Catholic: while we venerate the Pope as the Patriarch of the West, and thus **our** patriarch, the Faith that we see in History tells us that he is the first bishop among brother bishops, not as a monarch over them.[1] Neither can we accept that all Roman Catholic beliefs are part of the Ancient Catholic Faith.

---

[1] VIIth Council of Carthage (AD258) under St Cyprian: "For neither does any of us set himself up as a bishop of bishops, nor by tyrannical terror does any compel his colleague to the necessity of obedience; since every bishop, according to the allowance of his liberty and power, has his own proper right of judgment, and can no more be judged by another than he himself can judge another."

In our understanding, "Catholic" is not the same as "Roman Catholic." We will come back to that point later when we discuss what we mean by Catholic.

We're not the Church of England: while much of our history is common with the Established Church in the United Kingdom, their understanding of how the Church relates to Society is different from ours. They believe that the Christian Faith can and should adapt to fit the understanding of the society around them. We believe that the Christian Faith cannot change in such a way, but rather issues a challenge to everyone to be faithful to God and thus bring a greater sense of His Love in the world on His terms and not ours.

We are a tiny church, and many would regard us as being eccentric and a little bit awkward, but we have life-changing beliefs which we largely have in common with all Catholic Churches. Our sole purpose is to spread the Good News of Christ's love through the Ancient Catholic Faith once received by the Twelve Disciples, and to help guide people in living out that very faith. This includes you.

Exercise 1.2

What do you want the Anglican Catholic Church to do for you? What are your expectations of us? Discuss these with your Mentor. How might they answer the same questions?

You will probably now have more questions than answers. That's healthy: we cannot expect all our questions to be answered at once. Indeed, we will probably spend most of our lives asking the same questions and never find a satisfactory answer. This little guide will show you how we, the Anglican Catholic Church begin when we have difficult questions. It probably won't answer all your questions but we hope it will set you on the road to discovery. One good question to start with is, "Who is God?"

Chapter 2: Who is God?

We begin to look at what the Church believes. To do so, we must start looking at what the Church proclaims in the most important statement of Faith that we recite each Sunday at Mass.

The Nicene Creed

> I believe in one God, the Father Almighty, Maker of heaven and earth, and of all things visible and invisible.
>
> And in one Lord Jesus Christ, the only-begotten Son of God, begotten of the Father before all worlds; God of God, Light of Light, very God of very God; begotten, not made, being of one substance with the Father, by whom all things were made.
>
> Who, for us men and for our salvation, came down from heaven, and was incarnate by the Holy Ghost of the virgin Mary, and was made man; and was crucified also for us under Pontius Pilate; He suffered and was buried; and the third day He rose again, according to the Scriptures; and ascended into heaven, and sitteth on the right hand of the Father; and He shall come again, with glory, to judge both the quick and the dead; whose kingdom shall have no end.
>
> And I believe in the Holy Ghost, the Lord and Giver of Life; who proceedeth from the Father [and the Son]; who with the Father and the Son together is worshipped and glorified; who spake by the prophets.
>
> And I believe one holy catholic and apostolic Church. I acknowledge one baptism for the remission of sins; and I look for the resurrection of the dead, and the life of the world to come. Amen.

This Creed is the basis of our faith. There are two other creeds that we affirm: the Apostles' Creed is an abbreviation of the Nicene Creed and can be heard at Mattins and Evensong; the Athanasian Creed expands what we understand by the Holy Trinity. It is a longer creed than the Nicene Creed, but is still read regularly during the Church Year. There are no other Christian Creeds which speak about the faith as fully, or as truthfully as these three. We have included the Apostles' and Athanasian Creed in the Appendix.

Exercise 2.1

Read the Apostles' Creed and the Athanasian Creed. Note how they are different and, yet, note how they are saying the same things.

I believe

To believe literally means to hold something beloved. We say that we believe in our best friend when we trust them not to hurt us. We say that we believe in our husband or wife when we make our marriage vows and promise to keep them. We say that we believe in free health care, or in the right to free speech, if we hold these principles so strongly that we build our lives around that belief. Beliefs grow and change with us, but we may still hold onto them with the same sense of conviction. When we say that we believe it will rain tomorrow, what we are really saying is that we believe in our understanding of how nature works. We might be wrong, but that we are willing to trust in the way things appear to be working. When we cannot be absolutely certain, we must rely on our beliefs.

Exercise 2.2

What would you say that you believe in right now? How does it affect your life? Discuss this with your Mentor.

As Christians, we say that we believe in God. This Creed above sets out what that belief means. We may not understand it, but we don't have to. Our beliefs will develop and grow the more we try to understand. We just have to allow what we believe to change our lives, slowly but surely, in our own time. There will be many things that challenge our belief, but we should meet that challenge head on with honesty and see just how our belief meets that challenge. The Christian Faith is being challenged every day. However, the Church exists to be with you on your journey and to benefit from your membership too.

I believe in one God, the Father Almighty

Fundamentally, Christians first believe in only one God. God first revealed Himself to humanity – we did not find Him! – and the Old Testament is the testimony of the Hebrews who first saw Who God is. Read this excerpt from the third chapter of the book of Exodus about how one man, Moses, came to meet with God:

> Now Moses kept the flock of Jethro his father in law, the priest of Midian: and he led the flock to the backside of the desert, and came to the mountain of God, even to Horeb. And the angel of the LORD appeared unto him in a flame of fire out of the midst of a bush: and he looked, and, behold, the bush burned with fire, and the bush was not consumed. And Moses said, I will now turn aside, and see this great sight, why the bush is not burnt. And when the LORD saw that he turned aside to see, God called unto him out of the midst of the bush, and said, "Moses, Moses." And he said, "Here am I." And He said, "Draw not nigh hither: put off thy shoes from off thy feet, for the place whereon thou standest is holy ground." Moreover He said, "I am the God of thy father, the God of Abraham, the God of Isaac, and the

God of Jacob." And Moses hid his face; for he was afraid to look upon God.[2]

There are two things we know about God. First that He is a Father. You can only ever become a father by having children. The trouble is that some people want to be called "Father" to be important. In this sense, Jesus says, "call no man your father upon the earth: for one is your Father, which is in heaven"[3]. We call priests "Father" not because they are more important than anyone else, but because they are commanded to act as a father to their parish and because they are called to represent God who is our Heavenly Father. A good priest will take this duty very, very seriously or risk endangering his very soul.

Exercise 2.3
What should a good father be like?

It is the duty of a father to care for his children to the utmost, even to the giving up of his life for them. Sadly, there are many fathers today who are absent from their children for whatever reason. Even worse, there are some fathers who abuse their children. It is understandable, then, that many people can have a very negative view of what it means to be a father.

However, God is not just a father, He is the Father Almighty and therefore better than even the best human father can be. He is more reliable, more trustworthy and more loving, and He is Almighty. A famous hymn we sing says, "Ponder anew what the Almighty can do, if with his love he befriend thee."[4]

---

[2] Exodus iii.1-6
[3] St Matthew xxiii.9
[4] From *Praise to the Lord, the Almighty, the King of Creation* by J. Neander tr C. Winkworth

Exercise 2.4

What does Almighty mean to you? What can something Almighty do?

Maker of Heaven and Earth, and of all things visible and invisible

God is Almighty in the sense that everything that has come into existence depends entirely on Him for that existence. God brings everything we experience in our lives into being.

Exercise 2.5

Read the first chapter of Genesis. What do you hear?

Whether you believe it to be literally true or a poetic story, the first two chapters of Genesis tell the theological truth that God has created the Heavens and the Earth. We will discuss what we mean by theological truth later but in whatever way we read this famous passage of the Bible, we cannot escape the message that whatever exists, God created it. It might be visible like the sun, the sea, the trees, et c, or it might be invisible like atoms, the air, the laws of physics, thoughts, or even the angels.

St Paul says to the Colossians, "For by Him were all things created, that are in heaven, and that are in earth, visible and invisible, whether they be thrones, or dominions, or principalities, or powers: all things were created by Him, and for Him:"[5]

There are no such things as square circles, or rocks too heavy for God to lift – they cannot possibly exist. But we believe that God does exist, and that He has somehow caused everything to exist.

---

[5] Colossians i.16

This doesn't go against what Science says; in fact, it supports what Science says. Science says **how** things exist: God is the reason **why** things exist in the first place. He is why there is something rather than nothing.

This also means that God is the Creator of Time and Space and therefore completely free of them. This means that you cannot point to where God is, nor can you say how old God is. You might as well ask what is North of the North Pole, or what colour the number three was last February 30th.

And in one Lord Jesus Christ,

> "...the only-begotten Son of God, begotten of the Father before all worlds; God of God, Light of Light, very God of very God; begotten, not made, being of one substance with the Father, by whom all things were made."

We saw earlier that if God is a Father then He must have a child. You might think that we are His children and indeed we are but only, as St Paul says, by adoption. God is very, very different from us, and so we can't claim to be children of God naturally. There must be something more to being a natural child of God. This is where we really begin to explore what it means to be Christian. We believe, categorically, that Jesus Christ is the Son of God.

Exercise 2.6
What makes a good child?

In the early part of Christian history, a priest named Arius made the claim that Jesus is just a person created by God like we are, but with a special significance. This caused a lot of arguments among Christians. However, in AD 325, roughly three-hundred bishops from all around the Christian world met to discuss this question, and (after a lot of arguing as well as prayer and study) showed that the Bible tells us categorically that Jesus was not created, but begotten.

Exercise 2.7

Read the first chapter of the Gospel of St John[6] at least twice. What is it saying?

We often say that a son has the same bloodline as his father. What does this mean? It means that the son has something substantial in common with his father: the old language calls this begetting. This means that the Son of God must have the same substance as God the Father. This Son is the Word that St John's gospel is talking about, and we read that "the Word was God"[7]. Also, later on, Jesus cries out to God saying, "And now, O Father, glorify Thou Me with Thine own self with the glory which I had with thee before the world was."[8]

This is where we begin to encounter God as a Trinity. It is a supremely difficult topic because it is where God goes above all earthly thought. Christians believe in only One God. We have seen that the Father is God, and now we are told that the Word, i.e. the Son, is God as well. They are not the same persons, but they are both God - not parts of God. The Father is fully God (very God), and the Son is fully God (very God). We have just seen that God is at least two persons. We shall see that God is three persons, thus comprising the Trinity.

There are lots of analogies as to how God can be a Trinity, but they all fail. This is because God is unique. There is nothing else like Him, certainly not in Creation. Therefore we must be

---

[6] St John i
[7] St John i.1
[8] St John xvii.5

satisfied with being confused and simply believe that this is true. We can try to understand, but it is better to try and know God.

Exercise 2.8

If you find the idea of the Holy Trinity confusing, or even upsetting, pray to God this prayer:

Almighty God,
Three persons, One God,
I cannot understand how you exist,
but I do believe that you exist.
Help me, then, to know You better as I live my life with You.
Help me to glory in the fact that You go far beyond Man's understanding,
and give me peace of mind that I may worship You in spirit and in truth,
through the same Jesus Christ, Your Son, Our Lord,
Who lives and reigns with You,
in the unity of the Holy Ghost,
ever One God, world without end.
Amen.

Who, for us men and for our salvation,

> ...came down from heaven, and was incarnate by the Holy Spirit of the Virgin Mary, and was made man;

As we progress through the Creed, we come to a startling fact that is also very difficult to understand in its entirety, but is absolutely fundamental to our Faith. As St John says, "The Word was made flesh and dwelt among us."[9] We believe that the Son of God emptied Himself of His being God and became a human being just like us in every way except without sin. This is how God is able to communicate best with Human Beings, by becoming a

---

[9] St John i.14

Human Being. In the second chapter of his letter to the Philippians, St Paul says:

> Let this mind be in you, which was also in Christ Jesus: Who, being in the form of God, thought it not robbery to be equal with God: But made himself of no reputation, and took upon him the form of a servant, and was made in the likeness of men: And being found in fashion as a man, he humbled himself, and became obedient unto death, even the death of the cross. Wherefore God also hath highly exalted him, and given him a name which is above every name: That at the name of Jesus every knee should bow, of things in heaven, and things in earth, and things under the earth; And that every tongue should confess that Jesus Christ is Lord, to the glory of God the Father.[10]

This brings us to another problem that the Church had in the early years. Is Jesus God or is He man? The Appollinarians and Docetists thought the Jesus only appears to be human. The Nestorians thought that Jesus's humanity is completely separate from His divinity (His being God). These ideas contradict the fact that the Word became flesh. The Church believes that Jesus is both fully human and fully God, and cannot be separated, just like a human being can't remain human if their skeleton and flesh are separated. Of course, this is still difficult to understand. Nestorius believed that the Virgin Mary had only given birth to the human bit of Jesus, in which case God can't have been made man!

We know that Mary is the mother of Jesus, and that Jesus is fully God. Therefore, Mary is rightly called the Mother of God. This has

---

[10] Philippians ii.5-11

profound implications for who Mary is, as we shall explore a bit later.

Exercise 2.9
Why do you think that it is important for Jesus to be both a man and God?

And was crucified also for us under Pontius Pilate; He suffered and was buried;

The sixteenth verse of the third chapter of the Gospel of St John says:

> For God so loved the world, that he gave his only begotten Son, that whosoever believeth in him should not perish, but have everlasting life.[11]

In this we read why Jesus became a man.

Exercise 2.10
How would you summarise the life of Jesus?

The fact that the Roman Governor of Judaea is mentioned shows us that we are dealing with historical facts, not a story, nor a myth. This Jesus really exists, really teaches, and is really crucified to death under Pontius Pilate. There are many people today who say that Jesus never existed, but most historians are convinced that there is more good evidence for the existence of Jesus than for other historical figures like Julius Caesar or Socrates.

In his first letter to St Timothy, St Paul explains, "This is a faithful saying, and worthy of all acceptation, that Christ Jesus came into the world to save sinners; of whom I am chief."[12] Jesus comes into the world so that by His sacrifice of Himself on the Cross, He

---
[11] St John iii.16
[12] I Timothy i.15

might save us all from our sins. We will look at the nature of sin later, but we needed to be rescued from sin so that we might be saved from Death.

Exercise 2.11

Find out the difference between a contract and a covenant.

In the Old Testament, the relationship between God and Man was sealed with sacrifices. A sacrifice is something which is important to us that we give up to God to show that He is more important, and thus make it holy. We'll see more about what "holy" means later. Covenants were sealed in the blood of a sacrifice to show how important the Covenant was. The Old Covenant between God and man was that there should be a binding relationship between Israel and God which is sealed through the sacrificial system. In this system of sacrifices, people sacrificed some of their best and most expensive animals to God just to show how much they valued the covenant with Him.

At His Crucifixion, Jesus offers Himself to God as a sacrifice to seal a new covenant with Him. It is something He chooses willingly to do. Since He is man, Jesus' sacrifice of His very life is acceptable and appropriate to bring all human beings back into an intimate relationship with God. Since He is God, this sacrifice spreads out throughout all of Time for all human beings. This sacrifice we present again every week at the Mass. It is not a different sacrifice each week, but the same sacrifice for all time. We will come back to this issue, but this is why Anglican Catholics do not believe that the Christian Faith can change over time. The same sacrifice does for all people, everywhere, regardless of who they are, where they are, or when they are. All can be saved through the blood of Jesus Christ if they want to be. However, we don't get to change the system!

The Church remembers the Crucifixion most especially in the Sacred Triduum, the three days beginning in the Evening of Maundy Thursday. This is a very solemn time of the year, and was used as a time of fasting for those coming to be Baptised on Easter Day. We will discuss the Church year later.

And the third day He rose again, according to the Scriptures;

Again, we are faced with an historical fact. On the third day after He was Crucified, Jesus' tomb was empty. Further, people were saying that they had seen Him walking about, and that He was not a ghost.[13]

Exercise 2.12

Read the account of Jesus resurrection in the twenty-fourth chapter of St Luke's Gospel.

In his first letter, St Peter says,

> Blessed be the God and Father of our Lord Jesus Christ, which according to his abundant mercy hath begotten us again unto a lively hope by the resurrection of Jesus Christ from the dead, To an inheritance incorruptible, and undefiled, and that fadeth not away, reserved in heaven for you, Who are kept by the power of God through faith unto salvation ready to be revealed in the last time.[14]

We see the power of Jesus' resurrection from the dead. Jesus tells us that He is the Way, the Truth and the Life. In Him, humanity once separated from God by sin, is reconciled fully. St Athanasius tells us that "God became man so that man could become God."[15] Again, we see that Jesus has to be inseparably God and Man for

---

[13] E.g. St Luke xxiv.36-42
[14] I Peter i.3-5
[15] St Athanasius *On the Incarnation* liv.3

this to work. This is how He is the Way to being reconciled with God, the Truth that God and Man can be reconciled and the Life whereby we may have the opportunity to live a life beyond our little stretch of time in this world, a Life that is full and glorious, a life like God's.

Exercise 2.13
Read the fifteenth Chapter of St Paul's first letter to the Corinthians. [16] *How important is it that we believe in the Resurrection?*

The Church celebrates the Resurrection most especially on Easter Day. Traditionally, on this day, people were Baptised after a long period of preparation.

And ascended into heaven,
The trouble with being a human being is that you are limited to Time and Space. This is significant because we said earlier that God was independent of Time and Space. Yet, as a human being He makes Himself depend on Time and Space. We know that Jesus lives in Galilee in the First Century AD and is thus limited as a human being to this time and place. The trouble with limiting yourself means that you cannot do all that you necessarily want to do. Paradoxically, this means that Jesus has to leave us in order to be with us always even unto the end of the age.[17]

Exercise 2.14
Read the first eleven verses of the first chapter of Acts.[18]

---

[16] I Corinthians xv
[17] St Matthew xxviii.20
[18] Acts i.1-11

We see that Jesus' divinity does not change His humanity. He is still like us. Yet, because He is God, His humanity has the gift of not being dependent on Time and Space. It is because He has ascended that Jesus can now be present in every Catholic Mass.

He also promises that, once He is ascended, He will send the Holy Ghost to us. The Church celebrates the Ascension forty days after Easter. In the Anglican Catholic Church, this is always a Thursday.

And sitteth on the right hand of the Father;

> ...and He shall come again, with glory, to judge the quick and the dead; Whose kingdom shall have no end.

In the seventh chapter of the Book of Daniel, we read:

> I saw in the night visions, and, behold, one like the Son of man came with the clouds of heaven, and came to the Ancient of days, and they brought him near before him. And there was given him dominion, and glory, and a kingdom, that all people, nations, and languages, should serve him: his dominion is an everlasting dominion, which shall not pass away, and his kingdom that which shall not be destroyed.[19]

Here we see what is happening in Heaven immediately after the Ascension of Jesus that we saw in the first chapter of Acts. We see the fact that Jesus is enthroned as a King.

Exercise 2.15
What is a good king? How should a good king rule?

In order to be a king in the first place, you need to people to agree that you have the authority to be a king. Your kingdom is then formed of all those people who agree that you are a king. Jesus

---

[19] Daniel vii.13-14

speaks a lot about the Kingdom of God. We are told that Jesus' kingdom will never pass away.

We also believe Jesus when He says that He will return. In the fourteenth chapter of the Gospel of St John, Jesus says:

> Yet a little while, and the world seeth me no more; but ye see me: because I live, ye shall live also. At that day ye shall know that I am in my Father, and ye in me, and I in you.[20]

Many people look out for His return, and get carried away with themselves and issue dates and times of when this will be. But Jesus categorically says, "But of that day and hour knoweth no man, no, not the angels of heaven, but my Father only."[21] As a human being, Jesus does not know the hour of his return, but as God He does. This has big implications for Christians because we are also told that He will come like a thief in the night. We need to be ready for Him to return at any hour

Exercise 2.16

Read the twenty-fifth chapter of St Matthew's Gospel.[22] *What do you learn about the return of Jesus, and of His Kingdom? Do you really want to accept Jesus as your king?*

And I believe in the Holy Ghost, The Lord and Giver of Life;

Before He goes to His death, Jesus says to His disciples:

> If ye love me, keep my commandments. And I will pray the Father, and he shall give you another Comforter,

---

[20] St John xiv.19-20
[21] St Matthew xxiv.36
[22] St Matthew xxv

that he may abide with you for ever; Even the Spirit of truth; whom the world cannot receive, because it seeth him not, neither knoweth him: but ye know him; for he dwelleth with you, and shall be in you.[23]

The word "Comforter" literally means one who comes with strength for you. The word in Greek gives us the word Paraclete meaning one who comes alongside to help. This is not an angel, but the Spirit of truth. Remember what you read in the first chapter of Genesis? Right there in the very beginning, "the Spirit of God moved upon the face of the waters".[24] This is the Holy Spirit or Holy Ghost as we often call Him in the old language.

After reading through the Scriptures carefully, the Church soon realised that the Holy Ghost is not a thing, but a person in exactly the same way that God the Father is a person, and God the Son is a person.

Exercise 2.17

Read the twelfth chapter of St Paul's first letter to the Corinthians.[25] Does this help you decide whether the Holy Spirit is like the Father and the Son?

In the eighth chapter of the Book of Acts, it is the Holy Ghost who tells Philip to meet a particular chariot.[26] In the second and third chapters of the Book of Revelation, it is the Holy Spirit who speaks to the Churches.[27] And right at the end of the Bible in the twenty-second chapter of the Book of Revelation, the Holy Spirit with the Bride (which means the Church) call out to human beings to come and receive Eternal Life. All of this goes to show that the Holy Ghost can make decisions, speak His words and

---

[23] St John xiv.15-17
[24] Genesis i.2
[25] 1 Corinthians xii
[26] Acts viii.29
[27] Revelation ii-iii

draw people to Him. It is clear that the Holy Ghost is a person, not some mysterious force as some people might believe.

Exercise 2.18

Pray this prayer. If you can find the music of this written by Thomas Tallis, pray along with it!

*O Lord give Thy Holy Spirit into our hearts,
and lighten our understanding
that we may walk in the fear of Thy name all the days of our life;
that we may know Thee, the only true God,
and Jesus Christ Whom Thou hast sent.
Amen.*

Who proceedeth from the Father [and the Son],

> ...who with the Father and the Son together is worshipped and glorified;

We have seen that Jesus, the Son of God, is begotten of the Father. We have seen that He is fully God and fully Human. What can be said of the Holy Ghost? We have seen that the Holy Spirit isn't just an aimless energy directed by God, but a person too.

Jesus says "when the Comforter is come, whom I will send unto you from the Father, even the Spirit of truth, which proceedeth from the Father, he shall testify of me."[28] Just as the Son is begotten of the Father from Eternity, so the Holy Ghost proceeds from the Father through the Son from Eternity.[29] The Father is

---

[28] St John xv.26
[29] E.g Tertullian *Against Praxeas* iv.1 and St John Damascene *An Exposition of the Orthodox Faith Book I.xii.*

the source of the being of the Son, and the Holy Ghost: that is how He is the Father.

When the Nicene Creed was first completed in the fifth century, it said that the Holy Ghost proceeds from the Father. Later, an amendment was made to say that the Holy Ghost proceeds from the Father and the Son, but this amendment was not made with the full agreement of all the churches, especially the Eastern Orthodox Church which rejects it to this day. As Anglican Catholics, we are free to say the Creed with or without the words "and the Son" when discussing the procession of the Holy Spirit, provided that we mean that the Holy Ghost proceeds from the Father through the Son. In an ideal world, we should not say "and the Son" at all, and when the Anglican Catholic Church is big enough to have a full scholarly Council on the subject, those words will probably be removed from the Book of Common Prayer.

This all sounds rather irrelevant and even a bit pernickety, but the point is this. The Son is begotten of the Father: this means that the Son is God. Likewise, the Holy Ghost proceeds from the Father: this means that the Holy Ghost must also be God. In the tenth chapter of the letter to the Hebrews, we read

> Whereof the Holy Ghost also is a witness to us: for after that he had said before, This is the covenant that I will make with them after those days, saith the Lord, I will put my laws into their hearts, and in their minds will I write them; And their sins and iniquities will I remember no more.[30]

Notice that it is the Holy Ghost speaking, calling Himself "the Lord" and forgiving sins and iniquities. The only one who can do

---

[30] Hebrews x.15-17

all that is God. We have now fully discussed the teaching of the Church on the Holy Trinity.

Exercise 2.19

Read the sixth chapter of Isaiah[31] and the fourth chapter of the book of Revelation.[32] Can you find references to the Holy Trinity in these visions? What about in the eighteenth chapter of Genesis?[33]

Who spake by the prophets.

Throughout the Old Testament, the Holy Ghost has been active in inspiring the Prophets. Before the Gospels were being written down, St Paul says, "All scripture is given by inspiration of God, and is profitable for doctrine, for reproof, for correction, for instruction in righteousness."[34] Literally, all of the Old Testament that St Paul knew, and now the New to which he contributed majorly, is inspired (that is breathed out) by God. The Holy Ghost is known as the Breath of God since, in both Hebrew and in Greek, the word for "spirit" is the same as the word for "breath."

Exercise 2.20

Read the account of the descent of the Holy Ghost in the second chapter of Acts.[35] Do you think that the Holy Spirit descends on us, today?

The Holy Ghost is not as well-known as the Father and the Son to many Christians. To other Christians, He is better known than the Father and the Son. The reason for this is that many people

---

[31] Isaiah vi
[32] Revelation iv
[33] Genesis xviii
[34] II Timothy iii.16
[35] Acts ii

think that the Holy Ghost makes people speak in other languages and causes the uproar that we read in the second chapter of Acts. You may have seen Pentecostals being "filled with the spirit."

All Christians are filled with the Holy Spirit at their Baptism, and this Spirit living in us is fanned into flame at Confirmation. We will look at that further, later on. However, being filled with the Holy Spirit does not prevent us from following liturgy and set prayers. In fact, St Paul says that in public prayer, we need to be ordered.[36] Our Liturgy that we use is mainly comprised of words from Scripture and from the Church, so we can say that our liturgy is itself inspired by the Holy Ghost. In private, though, we can and should learn to pray with the Holy Spirit personally.

Exercise 2.21
Read the fourteenth chapter of St Paul's first letter to the Corinthians.[37] How can we tell that the Holy Ghost is in our worship?

And I believe one
Our focus now changes from believing in God, to our relationship with the Church. Notice that instead of saying, "I believe in..." we say, "I believe..." The meaning is essentially the same, but the Church bears witness to the existence, work and love of God which we must believe if we wish to be Christian.

In the Creed, we say that we believe **one** Church, but there are many Churches, aren't there?

Exercise 2.21
How many different Churches can you name? Do they have something in common?

---

[36] I Corinthians xiv.33
[37] I Corinthians xiv

The sad fact of the matter is that disagreements about what the Church teaches have resulted in people leaving the Church, such as the Arians and Docetists as we mentioned above. Other disagreements within the Church have occurred due to differences in how we understand authority and law within the Church. We have said that we are not in communion with the Roman Catholic Church, nor with the Church of England, and this is a very sorry state of affairs. It is a Christian duty to pray for the unity of Christ's Church on His terms and His alone. Yet, in the fourth chapter of his letter to the Ephesians, St Paul says,

> I therefore, the prisoner of the Lord, beseech you that ye walk worthy of the vocation wherewith ye are called, with all lowliness and meekness, with longsuffering, forbearing one another in love; endeavouring to keep the unity of the Spirit in the bond of peace. There is one body, and one Spirit, even as ye are called in one hope of your calling; One Lord, one faith, one baptism, One God and Father of all, who is above all, and through all, and in you all.[38]

As far as God is concerned there is only One Church, and it is this Church that we must keep seeking actively to be part of. To be One Church does not mean necessarily that the Church must exist as just a single organisation, but it is Jesus who makes the Church One and will reveal that One Church in Eternity. Former Archbishop of Canterbury, Dr William Temple says "If we are in the Father and the Son, we shall certainly be one, and our unity will increase our effective influence in the world. But it is not our unity as such that has converting power; it is our incorporation

---

[38] Ephesians iv.1-6

into the true Vine as branches in which the divine life is flowing!"[39]

Dr Temple is referring to Jesus' words:

> I am the true vine, and my Father is the husbandman. Every branch in me that beareth not fruit he taketh away: and every branch that beareth fruit, he purgeth it, that it may bring forth more fruit. Now ye are clean through the word which I have spoken unto you. Abide in me, and I in you. As the branch cannot bear fruit of itself, except it abide in the vine; no more can ye, except ye abide in me. I am the vine, ye are the branches: He that abideth in me, and I in him, the same bringeth forth much fruit: for without me ye can do nothing. If a man abide not in me, he is cast forth as a branch, and is withered; and men gather them, and cast them into the fire, and they are burned. If ye abide in me, and my words abide in you, ye shall ask what ye will, and it shall be done unto you. Herein is my Father glorified, that ye bear much fruit; so shall ye be my disciples.[40]

Following Jesus's commands, we cannot criticise other Christians for being members of a particular Christian group, especially if we are not being sincere in our own expression of Christianity. It is for each of us to ensure that we are walking sincerely with Christ and encouraging others to do so. The History of the Church is full of bloody battles where one group has tried to coerce another group into believing the same thing, and this is to our great shame! There cannot be any Thought Police in the Church!

---

[39] Temple, William: Readings in St. John's Gospel (Macmillan, London, 1959). p. 327.
[40] St John xv.1-8

Exercise 2.22

Pray for the visible unity of God's Church, for persecuted Christians, and for all Christian leaders and leaders of Christians.

Holy

The word "Holy" means separated out for God and means the same thing as "sacred." We have seen that God is really not the same as anything that has been created; indeed, God is the only thing NOT to have been created. We can make things holy by separating them out especially for God's purposes. The process of making something holy is called sacrifice, sanctification, or hallowing (see below) – that's literally what the word means. This does mean that anything we make holy we have to give it up completely to God – we cannot take it back without desecrating it – that's literally what that word means, too!

Exercise 2.23

Read the first chapter of Leviticus[41] and see how the Jews were expected to treat their sacrifices. Which animals were sacrificed? Why these animals?

If we love God then, clearly, we offer Him the best of what we have in order to demonstrate our sincerity to follow Him, to be at one with Him. This is why sacrifices were offered as part of one's repentance for sin. They demonstrated that they were at one with God. This is why we offer the sacrifice of the Mass. The sacrifices of animals aren't good enough to reconcile us fully back to God: they cannot make us holy. Only God can do that, and this is why Our Lord Jesus Christ, being both God and Man becomes a

---

[41] Leviticus i

sacrifice that DOES make us Holy if we receive His body and blood in the Mass.

Exercise 2.24

Why do you think the Church is Holy?

You may have heard the word "ecclesiastic" meaning something to do with the Church. This comes from a Greek word for the Church, and it literally means "those who have been called out." The Church is comprised of those who have been called out from living a sinful life in the world and into living a life dedicated to God.

St Paul says to the Colossians:

> If ye then be risen with Christ, seek those things which are above, where Christ sitteth on the right hand of God. Set your affection on things above, not on things on the earth. For ye are dead, and your life is hid with Christ in God. When Christ, who is our life, shall appear, then shall ye also appear with him in glory.[42]

We are to be holy, and Jesus tells us that we need to leave all that we have in order to follow Him. If we cling on to Earthly things, then we cannot be separated from Earthly things and thus we cannot ever be Holy. This doesn't mean that we cannot use the things around us, but we cannot let our possessions possess us. We have to be able to let them go when God tells us to.

It has to be said that there are times when the Church doesn't appear very holy: in fact, she often appears the opposite. The trouble is that the Church is comprised of people who are sinful and fallen. However, the Church has within itself the means of reconciling us back to God. Those members of the Church who have passed away have passed to God and have become saints

---

[42] Colossians iii.1-4

fully and are now completely holy. This is the destiny of every member of the Church and those who stay members of the Church are assured of this salvation. More on that later.

Catholic
Exercise 2.25

Have you heard the expression, "he has catholic tastes"? What does it mean?

The word Catholic comes from a Greek word meaning "according to the whole" and many people are of the opinion that it means "general" or "universal," but that isn't quite what the word means. The precise use of the word "Catholic" is disputed between Christians. The Roman Catholic Church calls itself *The* Catholic Church, and the Orthodox Church also believes that it alone is Catholic. What do Anglican Catholics believe?

We are very close, if not identical, in our understanding with the Orthodox Church. What we understand to be Catholic is best expressed by St Vincent of Lerins who says,

> Now in the Catholic Church itself we take the greatest care to hold that which has been believed everywhere, always and by all. That is truly and properly 'Catholic,' as is shown by the very force and meaning of the word, which comprehends everything almost universally. We shall hold to this rule if we follow universality, antiquity, and consent. We shall follow universality if we acknowledge that one Faith to be true which the whole Church throughout the world confesses; antiquity if we in no wise depart from those interpretations which it is clear that our ancestors and fathers proclaimed; consent, if in antiquity itself we

keep following the definitions and opinions of all, or certainly nearly all, bishops and doctors alike.[43]

In other words, to be properly Catholic, we have to be talking about the whole Church, past, present, and future. This does mean that the Church of the future will cease to be Catholic if she does not have the same Faith as the Church of the past. Indeed, you remember from above that there is only one Church and that Church is formed by all Christians past, present, and future. It follows that the Church cannot change its mind about the teaching of Jesus: anyone who does cannot be Catholic.

It is of great importance that we try to hold the Faith of our Fathers.

Exercise 2.26
Find the hymn, "Faith of our Fathers." Sing it through, and think about what the words are saying. We cannot keep the Faith of our Fathers without God's help, so pray for the help to keep this wonderful Faith so that you can know Him better and recognise His love for you.

And apostolic Church.
Literally, an apostle is someone who is sent on a mission. For His ministry to continue on Earth, Our Lord chose twelve disciples, eleven of whom became apostles.

Exercise 2.27
Read the tenth chapter of St Matthew's Gospel.[44] Who were the twelve disciples? Who are the eleven apostles?

---

[43] St Vincent of Lerins *Commonitorium*
[44] St Matthew x

Of course, the lives of the original Apostles were mostly cut short by persecution, torture and death. Only St John lived to old age. How could the faith carry on to today without them?

St Paul says to the Ephesians:

> Now therefore ye are no more strangers and foreigners, but fellowcitizens with the saints, and of the household of God; And are built upon the foundation of the apostles and prophets, Jesus Christ himself being the chief corner stone; In whom all the building fitly framed together groweth unto an holy temple in the Lord: In whom ye also are builded together for an habitation of God through the Spirit.[45]

You've already seen that the Faith of the Church is found in the Old Testament (i.e. the prophets) and the New Testament (i.e. the apostles). The Apostles were the first bishops of the Church, and we read in the first chapter of Acts that they found an apostle/bishop to replace Judas who had come to a very unpleasant end. Apostles therefore produced new apostles to lead the Church. This process is called consecration, and it is a means by which new bishops are made in a line of succession that reaches back to the original Apostles. These successors are still with us today as our bishops, and they are duty bound to preserve the Catholic Faith that they received at their consecration. We explore this a little further when we talk about the sacrament of Holy Orders.

However, we believe in an Apostolic Church. This also means that every Christian is sent out to do God's work in the world. Every

---

[45] Ephesians ii.19-22

Christian is called to bring the blessings of Christ into the world, to share the Good News, and fight against Evil.

Exercise 2.28
How might you be an apostle?

I acknowledge one baptism for the remission of sins;

If you're getting ready for Baptism then, clearly, you have some belief that there is something called Baptism in the first place. But what is Baptism really for?

In the second chapter of Acts, St Peter preaches a sermon which causes some people to realise that they have played a part in crucifying Jesus. They turn to Peter and ask what they can do. St Peter answers:

> Repent, and be baptized every one of you in the name of Jesus Christ for the remission of sins, and ye shall receive the gift of the Holy Ghost. For the promise is unto you, and to your children, and to all that are afar off, even as many as the Lord our God shall call.[46]

Sin violates our side of the covenant, but the covenant is not a contract. The Blood of Jesus still seals the covenant, and God is willing to uphold His side of the agreement through His love for us. Baptism cleanses us of the sins that we have committed, and realigns our free-will by the Holy Ghost taking up residence within us. When we are baptised, not only do we have the power not to sin against God but also, should we sin after Baptism, we have recourse to confession, repentance, and re-admittance into the company of God.

---

[46] Acts ii.38-39

Exercise 2.29

Read the third chapter of Genesis. Who is to blame for mankind's fall from grace?

Sin literally means a missing of the mark. To know what sin is requires us to know what Good and Evil are. Goodness comes from the very nature of God, but to know what Good is means that we have to know also what is not Good. Evil is the absence of Good.

God created human beings to have a free-will. This means that God has allowed us to choose how we run our lives without Him forcing us to make choices. We can choose good or evil freely, but in order to know whether to make a choice to do good things, we must learn what good and evil are. This is why God has given the Jewish people The Law which was made up of the commandments. Notice that the Law itself only tells us what is good and evil: it can't make us do good or evil, nor can it save us when we do evil things. We need God to help us to do good because goodness comes only from God's very nature.

In order for us to be truly free, God permits evil things to happen, but does not actively want evil things to happen. It is more important for Him that human beings should be free and have the choice not to follow Him. As Richard Bach says, "If you love something set it free. If it comes back it's yours. If not, it was never meant to be." However, because such truly horrible and terrible things happen from the evil that happen due to humanity's inhumanity, we need Salvation from Evil clinging onto us forever. This is what is being offered to us through Christ.

St Paul says to the Colossians:

Beware lest any man spoil you through philosophy and vain deceit, after the tradition of men, after the rudiments of the world, and not after Christ. For in him dwelleth all the fulness of the Godhead bodily. And ye are complete in him, which is the head of all principality and power: In whom also ye are circumcised with the circumcision made without hands, in putting off the body of the sins of the flesh by the circumcision of Christ: Buried with him in baptism, wherein also ye are risen with him through the faith of the operation of God, who hath raised him from the dead. And you, being dead in your sins and the uncircumcision of your flesh, hath he quickened together with him, having forgiven you all trespasses.[47]

Baptism cleanses us from sin by uniting us with Christ. We therefore die with Him to sin, and rise with Him to a new life free from the effects of Evil.

Exercise 2.30
Ask your Mentor to show you how to make a self-examination for sin. Think about how you are going to make a good repentance of those sins you have committed, and think about how you might fight those sins which you commit regularly. Remember, if you confess your sins freely to Christ and trust in Him, you will be forgiven.

And I look for the resurrection of the dead,
It is rather ironic that Death is really a gift from God. When one is dead, the Evil of the world cannot hurt us any more – we suffer no more. To be dead in Christ means that we will also be raised with Him. In Exercise 2.13, you were asked how important the Resurrection of the Dead is. As you saw, if there is no resurrection, there is no point to having any faith whatsoever

---

[47] Colossians ii.8-13

because we will all die, regardless of one's belief, and thus all of the sufferings of Christians are pointless. Yet, we know Christ's resurrection to be an historical fact, so there will be a resurrection of the dead.

Exercise 2.31

You can imagine the world before you were born, and you can imagine the world after you have died. Can you imagine actually being dead? Reflect deep down in yourself. Do you feel completely mortal, or is there something within you that you feel will go on forever?

Which dead people will be raised?

When he stands before the Roman Governor Felix in the twenty-fourth chapter of Acts, St Paul says,

> But this I confess unto thee, that after the way which they call heresy, so worship I the God of my fathers, believing all things which are written in the law and in the prophets: And have hope toward God, which they themselves also allow, that there shall be a resurrection of the dead, both of the just and unjust.[48]

Everyone will be raised from the Dead! Why? There are many people who have escaped justice for their deeds since by dying, and God is a God of justice for all people. We cannot expect to get away with sin simply by dying!

---

[48] Acts xxiv.14-15

Exercise 2.32
Pray for all those who are dying right now. Pray that they may find God's peace in their last minutes and that they may find God's love in the Resurrection of the Dead.

And the life of the world to come. Amen.
What happens after Resurrection? For the one who receives God's salvation, there is an Eternal life with God.

Exercise 2.33
Read the twenty-first chapter of the Book of Revelation.[49] What does it describe?

What is fascinating is that many people think that when we die, we lose our bodies. The Risen Jesus has a body, and we shall be raised from the dead with our bodies. We will not become angels, because angels are not human beings but creatures of pure spirit. We will not spend our days sitting on clouds playing harps, but live a full life in the presence of God. We will discuss this more later when we talk about Heaven.

We have now finished our look about what the Christians believe based on the Nicene Creed. It has opened up some topics that we will discuss later, but this Creed really has shown us Who God is and what He has in store for us. It is our duty to make sure that our Christian Faith is lived out in accordance with our belief so that we may approach God and our fellow human beings with honesty, integrity, sincerity and, above all, true Christian love.

Exercise 2.34
Read the Nicene Creed in its entirety once more and think back over what you understand. Is there anything that you don't quite follow? If there is, then ask your Mentor to guide you, but

---

[49] Revelation xxi

remember, no-one has all the answers except God. Of course, perhaps you should ask Him first!

Chapter 3: How do I respond to God?

How do we respond to God Who first loves us? We are to love God with all our being and our neighbours as ourselves. The love of God is rooted in worship. We worship something if we give it the greatest value in our lives: the word worship is literally "worth-ship." We worship God by putting Him at the centre of our lives with the greatest value to us, even greater than the value of our lives. It takes a lot of work to worship God properly, but He is patient and will help us to do so.

God does not need our worship: we need to worship Him because He gives us value and He wants us to be with Him always. It is only by accepting Him that we can exist fully in the first place, not just as strange monkeys that live eighty years and then die, never to be seen again. In recognising our need to have Him at the centre of our lives, we free our lives from being completely ruined by others, by nature, and even by our own fault. We believe in a God who seeks to transform us from being things of earth, to being things like Himself! This is why we worship Him.

Below, we list ways of worshipping God. In each case, see how they take away the value from things and put that value straight on to God.

Prayer, Fasting and Giving Alms
Exercise 3.1
Read the sixth chapter of St Matthew's Gospel.[50] How does this influence you to adopt the Christian lifestyle?

The first duty of every Christian is to pray to God. The reason is very simple. If we are to forge a relationship with someone, we

---
[50] St Matthew vi

need to speak to them, interact with them, know their mind, their opinions, their ideas. We cannot expect to be hired for a job on the strength of our CV alone. We need to talk to our interviewer so that they can get to know us and we them. Therefore, we must always pray first so that we can be in a better position for finding God's will for us and the world. We will shortly look in detail at how Jesus tells us to pray in the Lord's Prayer.

Jesus also tells us that we have to practise fasting and abstinence. An abstinence is a reduction in the quality of what we eat. Usually this involves abstaining from meat, except traditionally fish, for example replacing a juicy steak dinner with a vegetarian lasagne. Ideally, it is better to go properly vegetarian. A fast is to reduce the quantity of what we eat.

Both fasts and abstinences are personal acts of devotion to the Lord and Jesus says that we should never perform a fast to impress people, but rather to keep it part of one's personal relationship with Him. Traditionally, Lent and Advent, being seasons of penitence, require fasting <u>and</u> abstinence, and on almost all Fridays of the year (your priest will tell you when this isn't the case) Christians practise abstinence in remembrance of the day of crucifixion. This is why people still eat fish on Friday even though they are not Christian. An Anglican Catholic should seek to include fasting and abstinence as part of one's personal devotion. It is also as good for the body as prayer is for the spirit!

Notice also, that one can express fasting by giving up an aspect of our lives for a while, such as watching television or sleeping late. One can also "fast" by taking up an appropriate activity which draws us closer to God, such as replacing watching television with reading *The Imitation of Christ* by Thomas a Kempis. If we choose this sort of fast, then we should make sure that we do so with the intention of letting go of earthly things in order to be closer to Heavenly things. However, we should try and practise abstinence with our food as the Church directs so that we play our part in the wider Christian community.

Also, since a Christian is always part of a community, we should seek to contribute actively to that community by donation of time and/or money – a practice which the Church calls almsgiving. Again, this should not be practised just to impress people, but rather for the sole intention of making our community better through God's blessing. As God has blessed us, so the Christian should distribute that blessing more widely especially to those in need. We worship God by seeking to be like Him: if He is generous, so must we be!

A good practice is to make a donation to the Church in the weekly collections, but also to choose one or two good charities to support. You can support any charity which upholds the moral standard of the Church, but check with your priest first!

Exercise 3.2

Prepare some thoughts as to how you are going to adopt a programme of prayer, fasting and almsgiving. Remember that you need to work within your means, so don't plan to do more than you can. Discuss your ideas with your Mentor.

Keeping the Commandments

As we have seen, God is good. In fact it is part of Who God is to be good. This means that living in a relationship with God, we must seek always to do what He wants, because what He wants is good – our good, and the good of every person in the world. Admittedly, it is often very difficult to see that goodness in every situation, but in those situations we must trust God precisely because we cannot see what is really happening.

Since God first loves us, we need to respond to that love, and therefore we need to know what we ought to do and make sure that we're not doing what we shouldn't be doing.

We have the famous Ten Commandments which God gives the Israelites through Moses in the twentieth chapter of Exodus:

> God spake all these words, saying, I am the LORD thy God, which have brought thee out of the land of Egypt, out of the house of bondage. Thou shalt have no other gods before me. Thou shalt not make unto thee any graven image, or any likeness of any thing that is in heaven above, or that is in the earth beneath, or that is in the water under the earth: Thou shalt not bow down thyself to them, nor serve them: for I the LORD thy God am a jealous God, visiting the iniquity of the fathers upon the children unto the third and fourth generation of them that hate me; And shewing mercy unto thousands of them that love me, and keep my commandments. Thou shalt not take the name of the LORD thy God in vain; for the LORD will not hold him guiltless that taketh his name in vain. Remember the sabbath day, to keep it holy. Six days shalt thou labour, and do all thy work: But the seventh day is the sabbath of the LORD thy God: in it thou shalt not do any work, thou, nor thy son, nor thy daughter, thy manservant, nor thy maidservant, nor thy cattle, nor thy stranger that is within thy gates: For in six days the LORD made heaven and earth, the sea, and all that in them is, and rested the seventh day: wherefore the LORD blessed the sabbath day, and hallowed it. Honour thy father and thy mother: that thy days may be long upon the land which the LORD thy God giveth thee. Thou shalt not kill. Thou shalt not commit adultery. Thou shalt not steal. Thou shalt not bear false witness against thy

neighbour. Thou shalt not covet thy neighbour's house, thou shalt not covet thy neighbour's wife, nor his manservant, nor his maidservant, nor his ox, nor his ass, nor any thing that is thy neighbour's.[51]

Jesus gives us a very short way of understanding what we should be doing. In St Matthew's Gospel, we read the Two Commandments of the Lord:

> Then one of them, which was a lawyer, asked him a question, tempting him, and saying, Master, which is the great commandment in the law? Jesus said unto him, Thou shalt love the Lord thy God with all thy heart, and with all thy soul, and with all thy mind. This is the first and great commandment. And the second is like unto it, Thou shalt love thy neighbour as thyself. On these two commandments hang all the law and the prophets.[52]

Exercise 3.3

How do the Ten Commandments compare with the Two Commandments that Jesus gives us?

It is important that we know both sets of commandments. The Ten Commandments are mostly DON'Ts while the Two Commandments are both MUSTs. However, it is important that we should not become too obsessed with what the commandments say. We must always look at the spirit of the commandments and what God intends by them, rather than just sticking to the letter of the law. St Paul says, "the letter [of the law] killeth, but the spirit giveth life."[53]

For example Jesus says,

---

[51] Exodus xx.1-17
[52] St Matthew xxii.35-40
[53] II Corinthians iii.6

> Ye have heard that it was said by them of old time, Thou shalt not kill; and whosoever shall kill shall be in danger of the judgment: But I say unto you, That whosoever is angry with his brother without a cause shall be in danger of the judgment: and whosoever shall say to his brother, Raca, shall be in danger of the council: but whosoever shall say, Thou fool, shall be in danger of hell fire. Therefore if thou bring thy gift to the altar, and there rememberest that thy brother hath ought against thee; Leave there thy gift before the altar, and go thy way ; first be reconciled to thy brother, and then come and offer thy gift. Agree with thine adversary quickly, whiles thou art in the way with him; lest at any time the adversary deliver thee to the judge, and the judge deliver thee to the officer, and thou be cast into prison. Verily I say unto thee, Thou shalt by no means come out thence, till thou hast paid the uttermost farthing.[54]

So "Thou shalt not kill" means more than just not bashing someone on the head. It means not even considering them to be a fool! It means seeking resolution of conflict, recognising the fact of human weakness, and thinking from the other's point of view.

Exercise 3.4

How might Jesus ask you to interpret the other commandments? What's the intention behind each of them?

Repentance

According to St Matthew, the first word that Jesus utters in His public ministry is "repent!"[55] The word literally means to turn

---

[54] St Matthew v.21-25
[55] St Matthew iv.17

one's mind around, like steering a ship and clearly refers to the way we live our lives.

We each have a moral compass, and it's a good idea to cultivate that imagery to help us understand what's happening.

Exercise 3.5
How does a compass work? How do you make one?

Through Baptism, the Christian has had the needle of her moral compass magnetised to point to Christ. This is one of the effects. Without God first giving us a clear moral direction, we have no idea as to where to point our moral compass at all. St Paul says, "All things are lawful unto me, but all things are not expedient: all things are lawful for me, but I will not be brought under the power of any."[56] This means that we human beings have the power to do anything that we want, but not everything is beneficial. We can do what we like, but we should not let ourselves become addicted to our own power. Without God, we have to choose our own morality, but that's incredibly difficult!

When we make wrong choices, when we sin, we make our moral compass less powerful, and we forget how to do good things. Every time we sin, we take ourselves further and further away from Christ, and thus further and further away from becoming like Him. Just as a magnet loses its magnetism every time it is beaten or dropped, so sin damages our relationship with Christ. He Himself urges us to be perfect, just as His Father in heaven is perfect.

We need therefore to repent, to change our mind. We need to see the sins that we do, say sorry, and then try to live our lives anew **without** that sin. Seeing that Jesus is the Way to Eternal Life, we

---

[56] I Corinthians vi.12

should rather want to die in our flesh than to sin against Him: sin is **that** serious!

This is not easy. Some sins we have in our lives are habitual: we do them again and again, and don't seem able to stop. Some temptations are just so difficult to overcome, and before we're really aware of it, we've sinned again!

In the seventh chapter of his letter to the Romans, St Paul laments bitterly:

> For we know that the law is spiritual: but I am carnal, sold under sin. For that which I do I allow not: for what I would, that do I not; but what I hate, that do I. If then I do that which I would not, I consent unto the law that it is good. Now then it is no more I that do it, but sin that dwelleth in me. For I know that in me (that is, in my flesh,) dwelleth no good thing: for to will is present with me; but how to perform that which is good I find not. For the good that I would I do not: but the evil which I would not, that I do. Now if I do that I would not, it is no more I that do it, but sin that dwelleth in me. I find then a law, that, when I would do good, evil is present with me. For I delight in the law of God after the inward man: But I see another law in my members, warring against the law of my mind, and bringing me into captivity to the law of sin which is in my members. O wretched man that I am! who shall deliver me from the body of this death?[57]

Even the saints struggle: they, too, tend not to do the things they should, and do the things that they shouldn't!

---

[57] Romans vii.14-24

However, we now find out why the Gospel really is good news, because St Paul continues:

> I thank God through Jesus Christ our Lord. So then with the mind I myself serve the law of God; but with the flesh the law of sin.[58]

This is how we overcome Sin's addiction. As anyone who has given up smoking or drinking will tell you, you mustn't focus on not smoking or not drinking – that only leads back to smoking and drinking again. We have to replace our addiction with something better. We have to look for something good to fill the void where we would usually be falling into sin. This is why Jesus says to us, "seek ye first the kingdom of God, and His righteousness".[59] If we put Jesus first, centring our lives on Him, then we are always re-magnetising our moral compass. In Jesus, we shall be saved from our sins.

Exercise 3.6
Think about your sins, particularly those that you keep committing. Pray for the grace always to seek first the kingdom of God and His righteousness. Then remember that, if you are truly sorry for all the things you've done wrong, God will forgive you without hesitation.

Reading the Bible
We seek the kingdom of God first by immersing ourselves in His word. We have to learn to hear Him speak and take careful note of what He says. The Bible tells us who God is; it shows us Humanity's turbulent relationship with Him; it shows us how the person of Jesus Christ seeks us out to save us. You can see how necessary it is for the Christian to know and read the Bible daily.

---

[58] Romans vii.25
[59] St Matthew vi.33

Exercise 3.7

What bits of the Bible do you know or have you read? Do you have a favourite verse or passage? Why?

The Christian believes that the Holy Scriptures – the Bible – contains everything that is theologically true. What does this mean? Think about this sentence:

"The long arm of the law caught up with Gerald."

Literally speaking, the law does not have an arm, but this sentence tells us a lot. First, it tells us the fact that Gerald was arrested and, presumably punished, for some crime. Secondly, it tells us that the law has a long reach – it applies everywhere. Thirdly, it tells us that the law does not seem to be escaped easily.

In the same way, the Christian reads the Bible for theological facts, reading what the text is really saying about our relationship with God. Sometimes, it isn't very clear. Sometimes, it seems deadly dull! Yet, every word in the Bible is there for a reason.

The Bible was put together by the Church. There were many letters, gospels and writings around in the first and second centuries, but the Church only chose to put together writings that were authentic, written as closely as possible to the time when Jesus has visibly walked with us, and supported by the testimony of eye-witnesses and the stories they told. Holy Scripture, then, is the first and best source of what we know to be true about God – it is the primary source of God's revelation of Himself to us.

It is therefore very important to ensure that we read the Bible daily, and study what it is teaching us. In the Anglican Catholic Church, we use the Authorised Version – the King James Bible – as our standard of worship, but in private study it is a good idea to use a modern translation as some passages can be very hard to understand. A good version is *The Orthodox Study Bible* which is an accurate translation of the ancient languages of Greek and Hebrew in which the Bible texts are written.

Exercise 3.8
Discuss with your Mentor how you plan to do your daily Scripture reading. Your Mentor will be able to help you find a suitable Lectionary – a plan for daily reading – which will help you in your study.

Good deeds

Let us be clear. We cannot earn our way into Heaven. Salvation is a free gift that comes from striving to live with God. We are being saved because God wants to save us and we have the faith that He will do so. However, we cannot have a true faith in God without doing good things. St James says:

> Yea, a man may say, Thou hast faith, and I have works: shew me thy faith without thy works, and I will shew thee my faith by my works. Thou believest that there is one God; thou doest well: the devils also believe, and tremble. But wilt thou know, O vain man, that faith without works is dead? Was not Abraham our father justified by works, when he had offered Isaac his son upon the altar? Seest thou how faith wrought with his works, and by works was faith made perfect?[60]

We need to take the work of the Church very seriously.

Traditionally, there are fourteen good deeds that we can do that will help our faith to grow and will benefit all mankind. These are the seven corporal works of mercy (i.e. those that meet people's physical needs) and the seven spiritual works of mercy (i.e. those

---

[60] James ii.18-22

that meet people's spiritual needs). These are not exhaustive but give a good guide as to the good things that we can do as Christians. Therefore, they should be interpreted figuratively as much as they are literally. One might seek to help those imprisoned in abusive relationships, or help people grieve for a lost love one. You can find these listed in the Appendix. You might consider dedicating some of your time to train for a particular work, but it is better to work up to doing something while you explore the work that God has for you. Take this one step at a time!

Exercise 3.9

Read through the Works of Mercy in the Appendix. Think about how you could perform these in your life. Is there anyone who could do with this sort of help now?

Committing to the Church and Living the Faith

The Two Commandments say that we should love God with every fibre of our being and with everything that we can do. We should put Him first in all things.

You will notice from the Two Commandments that the Lord gives us that we cannot see ourselves as being alone. We always have to have a sense of how we relate to the people around us. The Commandment says explicitly, "Love thy neighbour as thyself." How do we love?

Exercise 3.10

Read the thirteenth chapter of St Paul's first letter to the Corinthians. If possible, memorise it! What do you notice?

One of the most interesting things to notice about love is that it is not a feeling. We feel in love, but really it is an active act of the recognition that other people have a value all of their own. Love is really an intense desire for the genuine good of other people. Clearly the good that we should want for others is that good that comes from God's own nature.

This is hard to do on our own, and we should remember that God has given us the gift of the community of the Church to which we belong in order for us to love more. The Church is full of fallible human beings - all sinners! We need to recognise this when we struggle with loving other people. We belong fully to the Church by the grace of our Baptism, and we need to play our part in supporting the Church in its mission to reach out to every human being and offer them the love of God.

The work of the Church is precisely to bring human beings the good news about salvation from Sin and Evil, to pour out the grace of God upon the world, and to pray to God for the needs of the world. It is the job of every Christian to commit to this task. Members of the Church are called laity, and the work of prayer that they have to do is called liturgy. In the Anglican Catholic Church, we see liturgical prayer as a way of the church coming together to pray the same prayers to God in old words, so that we join, not only with Christian all around the world in the same prayers, but also throughout Time as well. Liturgical prayer has been written to maximise the unity of the Church, and many of the prayers that are said daily mean a great deal to those who say them. There is an old Latin phrase – *lex orandi, lex credendi* – which means how we pray affects what we believe. The Creeds are not just statements of what we believe, they are prayers which join us to the One True God. It is vital, then, that we meet together on Sundays for Mass, and pray the same prayers daily.

Exercise 3.11

Attend a service of Mattins or Evensong in your parish. If they aren't available publicly, ask your priest if you can pray Mattins or Evensong with them so you can encounter what the Church must do on a daily basis. Think about how you can contribute to this duty.

As we have seen, we need to support the Church financially. The traditional method is that of tithing – giving the first 10% of our income, even before tax. However, the amount you give must reflect your circumstances balanced with the depth of your love for the Church. Aside from finance, we need to attend and support the Mass as this is how we bring our prayers for the whole world together before God. We need to assist the Church in its growth and outreach.

Often, just as in any family, disagreements (sometimes bitter feuds!) do break out in the Church. It is vitally important to know that this is not God's will for the Church to be divided. We believe only in One Church, so all Christians are to be united with each other in the love of Christ. Do not lose hope because of the failings of human beings, but pray for the grace of God to rise above these disagreements remembering that each Christian will be united to Christ and to each other in the end.

We should listen to our own calling and offer our particular talents to the Church. Remember, we should not let the priest do all the hard work, but help him to serve the Church.

Exercise 3.12

Think about your particular talents. What might you have to offer the Church? Pray for continual guidance to hear God's will for your life.

In living our Christian lives in the world, it is important to get our hearts right with God. Jesus famously preaches the Sermon on the Mount which begins in the fifth chapter of St Matthew's Gospel. [61] It sets out how our hearts and intentions need to change in order to be blessed. Remember that blessing is a form of spiritual happiness, a happiness that everyone can have and which doesn't depend on any circumstance or accident of our lives. Everyone can be blessed by God whether they believe in Him or not. It is whether they wish to receive such happiness that is important as God will not force His love on those who do not wish to receive it.

The Sermon on the Mount has profound implications for the way a Christian should live. We've already seen some of these aspects.

Exercise 3.13
Read the fifth chapter of St Matthew's Gospel and reflect on your life. Pray that you may see how you can become more blessed in your life.

One thing Our Lord teaches us is how we should pray. We now turn to examine the Lord's Prayer and how this should guide our conversations with God.

Chapter 4: How do I talk with God?
Prayer in general
We should never be afraid to pray because we can't find the right words. St Paul reassures us that "the Spirit also helpeth our infirmities: for we know not what we should pray for as we ought:

---

[61] St Matthew v-vii

but the Spirit itself maketh intercession for us with groanings which cannot be uttered."[62]

We will look at prayer more in depth as we study the Lord's Prayer below, but do begin to think about how you can start your daily prayer life with God.

Exercise 4.1

Discuss with your Mentor how you can begin to say prayers daily. They will advise you on how to start. Remember, start gently and then build things up as you get used to prayer. We include some prayers in the Appendix below.

Our Father

The first word of the Lord's Prayer is "Our," not "My." This should be our first clue as to how we should pray. Ideally, Christians should pray together regularly. Jesus says, "if two of you shall agree on earth as touching any thing that they shall ask, it shall be done for them of my Father which is in heaven. For where two or three are gathered together in my name, there am I in the midst of them."[63] This doesn't mean that we cannot pray alone, but rather we should see our prayers as being in common with the whole Church. We can pray for our own needs confident that the whole Church is praying for us, but then we have to remember to return that favour and pray more readily for the intentions of others. We need to make sure that we are praying for all those in need, especially those we can name, for they truly are our neighbours!

---

[62] Romans viii.26
[63] St Matthew xviii.19-20

Exercise 4.2

Who should you be praying for regularly? Make a list (not too long) of those people who you think need your prayers.

The second thing we note is that God is our Father. We know that all human beings are related by being created by God, but God actively wants us to know Him as our Father – He is not just the Father of Jesus. That's the sort of relationship He wants with us. He wants us to see Him as having a sincere concern about what we want and need, that He cares about our lives and is seeking to bring us to perfection in Him.

This means that we are able to approach Him about anything, even things we're ashamed about, or find uncomfortable. His ear is always open to us.

Who art in Heaven

This is a mysterious statement. When we say "heaven" we usually look up to the sky. If we do look up to the sky, then we are faced with the vastness of space with all its planets, stars, comets, meteors, galaxies, clusters and superclusters. We find ourselves rushing beyond the confines of our little space, our home, our town, country and even planet. When we say "Our Father Who art in Heaven" we are looking to God Who is beyond anything we can possibly imagine. He is beyond space and time, always present at every stage of our lives. St Augustine says to God, "Thou wast more inward to me than my most inward part; and higher than my highest."[64]

---

[64] St Augustine *Confessions Book III*

Exercise 4.3

Read Psalm 139. Allow your mind to reflect on how small our Universe is compared with God and how well known you are to Him.

Hallowed be Thy name

When we regard something as being Holy, we hallow it. But isn't God's name already Holy? Why does it need to be hallowed by us?

Exercise 4.4

What things do you hallow? What do you regard as being particularly holy? Why?

You will know already that the Holy Name of Jesus is taken as a swear word today. People bandy about the word "God" with scant regard for its meaning or Who it's referring to. In short, many people do not regard the words used by the Church to be holy. There have been instances of people wandering into Masses and attacking the priest saying the Liturgy. Evil profanes, but Good hallows.

When we pray, "hallowed be thy name," we pray that the world will wake up to the fact that God exists and is truly holy. We are praying for the end of taking the Lord's name in vain, so that people can see the God Who loves them so completely that He gave His life for them so that they could be reconciled with Him.

We can do our bit too, by living out this prayer. We need to see things as holy in order to make God real. There is a good practice of bowing slightly when the Name of Jesus is mentioned. Watch for this in Church. The Bishop will nod, and priests doff their birettas (liturgical hats) whenever Jesus' name is mentioned.

Some priests will refer to Jesus only as Lord in order to respect the Holy Name.

Watch also for liturgical actions such as the priest kissing the altar or the Gospel book. The liturgy inspires us to learn respect for the Holiness of God. Every liturgical action has a meaning that is meant to draw us closer to God: it isn't done just to be fancy!

Exercise 4.5

Learn to bow your head at the name of Jesus. Also, watch for other ways that Christians seek to make God's name hallowed in the world, in the liturgy and outside.

Thy Kingdom come

The last Sunday in October is called Christ the King Sunday in which we pay special attention to Jesus as our King. As you saw in Exercise 2.16, Christians submit themselves to the Rule of Jesus as King. This doesn't mean that we reject earthly rulers – indeed St Paul tells the Romans:

> Let every soul be subject unto the higher powers; for there is no power but of God: the powers that be are ordained of God. Whosoever therefore resisteth the power resisteth the ordinance of God: and they that resist shall receive to themselves damnation. For rulers are not a terror to good works, but to the evil. Wilt thou then not be afraid of the power? do that which is good, and thou shalt have praise of the same: for he is the minister of God to thee for good. But if thou do that which is evil, be afraid; for he beareth not the sword in vain: for he is the minister of God, a revenger to execute wrath upon him that doeth evil. Wherefore ye must needs be subject, not only for wrath, but also for conscience sake. For for this cause pay ye tribute also; for they are God's ministers, attending continually upon this very thing. Render therefore to all their dues;

tribute to whom tribute is due, custom to whom custom, fear to whom fear, honour to whom honour.[65]

We are to respect earthly rulers because we submit to Christ who gives each earthly ruler the authority to rule. The trouble is that earthly rulers do not necessarily accept the Kingship of Christ, and History shows us of many atrocities brought about because of corrupt leaders and wicked rulers. When we pray, "Thy Kingdom come" we pray that everyone may accept the rule of Jesus as King so that acts of war, genocide, oppression, and cruelty may cease in all the world.

Exercise 4.6
Pray for the leaders of all countries, especially those whose policies are hurting innocent people.

Thy Will be done in Earth as it is in Heaven

We already know that Jesus is the King of Heaven, and that accepting Him as our King means that we want Him to be King on earth. If we accept this then we have to do what He tells us. We must seek His will in the world, starting in our own lives. Essentially, we have to build the Kingdom of Heaven here on Earth!

We see much in the world that we know is not God's will: murder, corruption, wealth hoarded so that others starve, children abused and even killed beneath our noses! Clearly, that must stop and it is down to us Christians to fight all Evil in God's name.

But we cannot do this of ourselves. If we think we know what we're doing, we can easily make things worse.

---

[65] Romans xiii.1-7

In the nineteenth chapter of the Acts we read:

> And God wrought special miracles by the hands of Paul: So that from his body were brought unto the sick handkerchiefs or aprons, and the diseases departed from them, and the evil spirits went out of them. Then certain of the vagabond Jews, exorcists, took upon them to call over them which had evil spirits the name of the Lord Jesus, saying, We adjure you by Jesus whom Paul preacheth. And there were seven sons of one Sceva, a Jew, and chief of the priests, which did so. And the evil spirit answered and said, Jesus I know, and Paul I know; but who are ye? And the man in whom the evil spirit was leaped on them, and overcame them, and prevailed against them, so that they fled out of that house naked and wounded. And this was known to all the Jews and Greeks also dwelling at Ephesus; and fear fell on them all, and the name of the Lord Jesus was magnified.[66]

If we don't do God's will then we could be contributing to Evil, not to Good. Therefore, we must pray to know God's will and then do that, just as He has it in Heaven.

Exercise 4.7
How do we discern God's will? Have we already discussed this to your satisfaction, or do you have more questions?

Give us this day our daily bread

We need God to give us all that we need from day to day. We pray for this because we need to recognise our complete dependence on Him. God promises to give us all that we need if we ask Him. In the eleventh chapter of St Luke's Gospel, we read that Jesus says:

---

[66] Acts xix.11-17

I say unto you, Ask, and it shall be given you; seek, and ye shall find; knock, and it shall be opened unto you. For every one that asketh receiveth; and he that seeketh findeth; and to him that knocketh it shall be opened. If a son shall ask bread of any of you that is a father, will he give him a stone? or if he ask a fish, will he for a fish give him a serpent? Or if he shall ask an egg, will he offer him a scorpion? If ye then, being evil, know how to give good gifts unto your children: how much more shall your heavenly Father give the Holy Spirit to them that ask him?[67]

Exercise 4.8

Identify in your life three things that you believe that you need God to provide for you. Now reflect on them carefully. How can you be sure that they are "I need"s and not "I want"s?

There is something more. The Greek word which we translate as "daily" really means something greater. As a word that is unique in the New Testament, it points us to the bread that exists beyond our understanding, and our limits of Space and Time. We will explore this further when we look at the Mass.

Notice that, as we say **Our** Father, so we speak of **our** daily bread. We are not to pray exclusively for ourselves, but for other people. As we will see, the saints in Heaven still pray for us. Our duty is to bring as many of the concerns of the world we know to God. That is called the priesthood of all believers, and you have already seen the ways in which this priesthood is worked out.

---

[67] St Luke xi.9-13

And forgive us our trespasses as we forgive those who trespass against us

We have seen that forgiveness is something that God readily offers us if we repent. What is forgiveness? We forgive when we put someone's sin aside, leave it behind, and move on together in reconciliation with a healed relationship. Essentially we forget – not that the sin ever happened, but rather that it doesn't matter anymore.

That's hard to do and we might be tempted not to forgive when someone hurts us horribly. But there is a problem. Jesus tells us a little parable:

> Therefore is the kingdom of heaven likened unto a certain king, which would take account of his servants. And when he had begun to reckon, one was brought unto him, which owed him ten thousand talents. But forasmuch as he had not to pay, his lord commanded him to be sold, and his wife, and children, and all that he had, and payment to be made. The servant therefore fell down, and worshipped him, saying, Lord, have patience with me, and I will pay thee all. Then the lord of that servant was moved with compassion, and loosed him, and forgave him the debt. But the same servant went out, and found one of his fellowservants, which owed him an hundred pence: and he laid hands on him, and took him by the throat, saying, Pay me that thou owest. And his fellowservant fell down at his feet, and besought him, saying, Have patience with me, and I will pay thee all. And he would not: but went and cast him into prison, till he should pay the debt. So when his fellowservants saw what was done, they were very sorry, and came and told unto their lord all that was done. Then his lord, after that he had called him, said unto him, O thou wicked servant, I forgave thee all that debt, because thou desiredst me: Shouldest not thou

also have had compassion on thy fellowservant, even as I had pity on thee? And his lord was wroth, and delivered him to the tormentors, till he should pay all that was due unto him. So likewise shall my heavenly Father do also unto you, if ye from your hearts forgive not every one his brother their trespasses.[68]

God wants us to be like Him, and He is forgiving in His nature. If we don't want to forgive, then we are actively saying that we don't want to be part of God's family. Forgiveness can be so hard, but it is possible. We have to remember that we all need to be transformed into the likeness of God. When we are raised from the Dead to live in God's kingdom, it is possible that our worst enemy will be there too. If we truly forgive, then we should want that to happen – we should want to be in Eternity with our worst enemy! Of course, both you and your worst enemy will be transformed and perfected in Christ, so this whole experience will not be horrible – unless you let it by not forgiving.

St Peter asks Jesus, "Lord, how oft shall my brother sin against me, and I forgive him? till seven times?" Jesus says to him, "I say not unto thee, Until seven times: but, Until seventy times seven"[69] – i.e. indefinitely: we need to keep forgiving for as long as it takes.

Exercise 4.9

Find and read the story of St Maria Goretti. Read also the account of the shooting of Pope St John Paul II. Do these inspire you to forgive others? If there is someone you cannot forgive at the moment, then pray for help to do so.

---

[68] St Matthew xviii.23-35
[69] St Matthew xviii.21-22

Remember, forgiveness does take time, just as wounds take time to heal – we just have to let the wounds heal and not open them up in any way!

And lead us not into temptation, but deliver us from Evil

Christians face temptation all the time. Even Jesus is tempted like we are, but He didn't sin.[70] Although He was tempted all through His life, we see His temptation most notably in St Luke's Gospel.[71]

Exercise 4.10
Read the fourth chapter of St Luke's Gospel. What does the Devil tempt Jesus with? How does he tempt Him?

Temptation is a very tricky thing to deal with. It isn't just about craving a cigarette or a seventeenth custard cream. Sometimes, temptation is very subtle and, before we know it, we can be caught off guard and find ourselves in sin. Yet, would God really lead us into temptation?

When we pray "Lead us not into temptation but deliver us from evil" we are recognising that we cannot stand up against sin, the world and the Devil without the assistance of Almighty God. We may want to do the will of God, but we also know that we shall fall. We pray for the strength to avoid temptation, to flee from those near occasions of sin, and, when tempted, to look honestly and earnestly for the will of God in that situation.

We pray that we may be delivered from evil, not that we won't feel the side-effects, but that we won't succumb to it. We are praying for the strength to trust God, even in the darkest, most wretched and miserable hour as we wrestle with the evils that beset us. Our deliverance from Evil IS our salvation which is being worked out

---

[70] Hebrews iv.15
[71] St Luke iv

now with God. That working out of our salvation comes with fear and trembling, but, recognising that God is there for us, anything against us will fall.

Exercise 4.11

How do you think that you are being tempted? Is it really as obvious as you think?

Amen

There is a word that we always end our prayers with, and yet we seem to treat it as a full-stop for prayer rather than considering that it has a very important and precise meaning. This word is "Amen." What does it mean?

It is a Hebrew word that means "so be it" or, as Captain Jean-Luc Picard might say, "make it so!" It is included at the end of liturgical prayer so that everyone present gives their agreement to what has been said. It is everyone's "yes" to what has been prayed.

However, in the third chapter of the Book of Revelation, Jesus says to St John, "And unto the angel of the church of the Laodiceans write; These things saith the Amen, the faithful and true witness, the beginning of the creation of God;..."[72] Jesus describes Himself as "The Amen." He is God's "yes!" to us. When we say, "Amen" we are becoming one with the Church. When Jesus says He is the Amen, He is uniting Himself with the Church too. In the imagery of the Book of Revelation, Jesus is the Bridegroom and the Church is the Bride, and this Amen is an expression of how humanity and God are united in Christ Jesus. This is a deep mystery and one worth thinking about.

---

[72] Revelation iii.14

Exercise 4.12

Can you train yourself to think of the whole Church saying "Amen" to your prayers? Can you train yourself to see yourself as part of the Church's "yes!" when you say "Amen" in the Liturgy?

The Intercession of the Saints

In the Apostles' Creed we say that we believe in the Communion of Saints. What does this mean? We have already said that we believe in One Church and that all Christian believers are united in this Church. Of course, most of those believers are no longer with us, and yet we know that we have Eternal life in Christ. This means that, essentially, all Christians who are with God in Heaven are still with us somehow! That's a deep mystery as to how that works, but it is at the heart of what Christians believe. We believe in the Resurrection of the Dead, and Eternal life with Christ.

In the twelfth chapter of the letter to the Hebrews, we read:

> Wherefore seeing we also are compassed about with so great a cloud of witnesses, let us lay aside every weight, and the sin which doth so easily beset us, and let us run with patience the race that is set before us, Looking unto Jesus the author and finisher of our faith; who for the joy that was set before him endured the cross, despising the shame, and is set down at the right hand of the throne of God.[73]

We can't be surrounded by witnesses if they are behind us in Time; they have to be with us now! These are the saints: the word saint means holy! These are the people in Eternity with God. We

---

[73] Hebrews xii.1-2

are in communion with them because they are united in Christ as we will be.

We cannot know in this life who is a saint, but the Church has been convinced that certain individuals have made it into Eternity with God. This is why we have St Peter, St Paul, St Matthew, St Mark, St Luke, St John, et c., because the Church believes that they are in Heaven praying for us.

Exercise 4.13

How many saints can you name? How many do you really know about?

If we still have fellowship with the saints, and if we are to become saints, and it is our duty to pray for everyone and support the Church, then it follows that the saints in Eternity can somehow pray for us in our lives on Earth. Indeed, in the fifth chapter of the Book of Revelation, we read:

> And when He [Jesus appearing symbolically as a lamb] had taken the book, the four beasts and four and twenty elders fell down before the Lamb, having every one of them harps, and golden vials full of odours, which are the prayers of saints.[74]

We often ask friends and family to pray for us when we are in need of prayers. We do so because we want their support and their solidarity as we go through difficult times. The same is true with the saints. We can ask them to pray for us. Whatever we are going through, the saints have gone through before. Some saints pray for particular things. St Lucy is the patron saint of those with eye-diseases. St George is the patron saint of England. St Isidore

---

[74] Revelation v.8

of Seville is the patron saint of the internet! We should not pray to them as if they will do something about it, but rather that they will support our prayers, and that the good that they did in their lifetime (which we call their merits) will help us to see the way through our lives. Saints are never to be worshipped, and they would abhor anyone bowing down to them as they should to God. However, a saint should be venerated as one would venerate a dignitary. These are people who have built up God's Church, so we should be grateful to them, and worship God because of them.

Getting to know a saint is a good idea, because their lives can show us how we might approach our own. There are many interesting lives, some of which ended in excruciating pain, which should encourage us. The merits of the saints in their lifetimes send ripples of God's Goodness through Time which also encourage us, and we can continue to spread that Good by following their examples. If we look to become saints, then we should do good things so that our merits today can support those in the Church's future.

Exercise 4.14
Do you have a saint that you would like to know more about? Do you have a patron saint? Find and pray the Litany of the Saints. If you have time, try and find out something of the lives of these people.

Praying for the Dead
If the saints pray for us, then death is not a barrier to our relationship with other members of the Church. We are One Church and therefore all in communion. This does mean that we are still in communion with all Christians who have died. This does mean that we are permitted to pray for the dead. In the Catholic Church, it is the practice to pray for the repose of the souls of those who have died. We pray for them so that we can

stand in solidarity with our deceased brothers and sisters as well as our brothers and sisters across the globe. We do not know precisely what effect this will have for them, but we can be assured that our prayers will assist them somehow.

The Church celebrates special Masses for the Dead called Requiem Masses. We also remember all the departed on All Souls' Day on 2nd November.

Exercise 4.15

If you don't already, do consider praying for those you know who have departed this life.

Chapter 5: How do I know Good and Evil?

It is important for us to know what Good and Evil are. If we read the third chapter of Genesis carefully, human beings stole the fruit of the knowledge of Good and Evil for themselves.[75] This means that human beings are tempted to make up their own ideas of what Good and Evil are rather than looking to God to tell them. Good is found in God's being: Evil is found in where He withdraws Himself. He withdraws Himself so that we might know Him better, and it is down to us to choose Him and His goodness rather than wander away into Evil and Darkness.

We shall look at seven examples of particular sins along with their "cures." They are classical examples which the Church Fathers have used as "primary colours" to show how they mix together to form all kinds of sin. Really, they are not meant to be an exhaustive list, but you can certainly see how they each affect our world today. It's actually quite a fun game to think about what happens when we mix two or three of them together, but it's all very serious when we realise how these affect us in our lives. With this in mind, we present the Seven Deadly Sins alongside the Seven Cardinal Virtues.

It's also worth bearing in mind that sin is our failure to worship God. Every sin is the result of us finding something more important in our lives than loving God, and so the cure will be giving God the value He deserves. Do remember that transforming our lives takes time – a lifetime – and God can forgive any sin that we repent of. Remember, also, that you are

---

[75] Genesis iii.6

not expected to master these virtues before your Baptism, Confirmation, or Reception. They are a matter of ongoing development for all Christians!

Gluttony versus Abstinence and Temperance

We often perceive gluttony as an over-indulgence with food. However, strictly speaking it is the preoccupation with having things just the way we like them. C.S. Lewis points out that the lady who wants just a little bit of toast but done a very specific way is just as gluttonous, if not more so, as someone who snaffles all the biscuits.[76] We suffer from gluttony when we have a desire to control our resources and to impress our will upon what we consume. Our focus becomes, not God, not even the good of ourselves, but rather the thing we want, the way we want it.

Actually, we have already discussed the cure for Gluttony. Practising fasting and abstinence for the love of God helps us detach our desires from what we consume and direct them to God. However, we must also remember that God does give us good food to enjoy – He is no ogre who would see us starve ourselves in some sort of appeasement to Him. In the first Chapter of Genesis, God sees all that He has made and says that it is very good!

St Paul says, "Whether therefore ye eat, or drink, or whatsoever ye do, do all to the glory of God."[77] This is why Christians say Grace before meals to give thanks to God for His provision. We also do well to eat whatever is set before us in a spirit of gratitude, no matter how well or badly it is cooked. If we deliberately hold

---

[76] C.S. Lewis *The Screwtape Letters*
[77] I Corinthians x.31

back from eating too much, then we are showing the virtue of Temperance which is often expressed through Abstinence.

We should also seek to keep ourselves heathy. St Paul says, "Know ye not that ye are the temple of God, and that the Spirit of God dwelleth in you?"[78] In showing Temperance, we are training ourselves by keeping ourselves healthy so that we can work to serve God as best we can. However, we do well not to become obsessed with our fitness – that way we fall into another sin!

Exercise 5.1
Reflect on your attitudes to food and drink, what you consume and how you consume it. How might you cultivate the virtue of temperance better?

Avarice versus Generosity

Avarice is the sin of hoarding things so that others cannot possess them. We can think of those infamous "fat cat" employers who pocket all the profits and pay a pittance to those who work for them. Avarice, again, demonstrates our desire to control not only what we have but also what we don't want other people to have. Why does a man seek to be rich if not to take complete control over his life and to protect himself from the demands of others on our lives?

Whereas Gluttony is the worship of things that we consume, Avarice is the worship of things that we collect. We may have in mind the character of Ebenezer Scrooge from Charles Dickens' *A Christmas Carol* or Shylock in *The Merchant of Venice* who values his ducats as much as (if not more than) his daughter![79]

We can see that avarice is a bit like a baby who will not share her toys with anyone. Babies, of course, are too little to understand

---

[78] I Corinthians iii.16
[79] William Shakespeare, *The Merchant of Venice* Act ii, Scene 8

what's going on and have to learn to give and take. Avarice is born of the fear that when something is taken away, it can't be replaced. We focus too much on the horror of losing something and thus ensure that we don't.

We can combat avarice by being generous with what we have. In the letter to the Hebrews, we read, "Let your conversation be without covetousness; and be content with such things as ye have: for he hath said, I will never leave thee, nor forsake thee."[80] Again, God gives us good things to enjoy, but not to replace Him.

In the nineteenth chapter of St Matthew's Gospel, we read:

> And, behold, one came and said unto him, Good Master, what good thing shall I do, that I may have eternal life? And He said unto him, Why callest thou me good? there is none good but one, that is, God: but if thou wilt enter into life, keep the commandments. He saith unto him, Which? Jesus said, thou shalt do no murder, thou shalt not commit adultery, thou shalt not steal, thou shalt not bear false witness, honour thy father and thy mother: and, thou shalt love thy neighbour as thyself. The young man saith unto Him, All these things have I kept from my youth up: what lack I yet? Jesus said unto him, If thou wilt be perfect, go and sell that thou hast, and give to the poor, and thou shalt have treasure in heaven: and come and follow me. But when the young man heard that saying, he went away sorrowful: for he had great possessions. Then said Jesus unto His disciples, Verily I say unto you, That a rich man shall hardly enter into the kingdom of heaven. And again I say unto you, It is

---

[80] Hebrews xiii.5

easier for a camel to go through the eye of a needle, than for a rich man to enter into the kingdom of God.

When his disciples heard it, they were exceedingly amazed, saying, Who then can be saved? But Jesus beheld them, and said unto them, With men this is impossible; but with God all things are possible. Then answered Peter and said unto Him, Behold, we have forsaken all, and followed Thee; what shall we have therefore? And Jesus said unto them, Verily I say unto you, That ye which have followed me, in the regeneration when the Son of man shall sit in the throne of his glory, ye also shall sit upon twelve thrones, judging the twelve tribes of Israel. And every one that hath forsaken houses, or brethren, or sisters, or father, or mother, or wife, or children, or lands, for my name's sake, shall receive an hundredfold, and shall inherit everlasting life. But many that are first shall be last; and the last shall be first.[81]

If we want to be perfect, then we should want to give up all that we have for Jesus. Literally giving up everything in one glorious gesture not quite what He requires (unless you're St Francis), but rather that we should learn to detach ourselves from our belongings. By being generous with what we have, we show God that we are concerned about the well-being of others and release ourselves from the fear that things will fall apart and decay. Like all the other virtues, Generosity is difficult to put into practice, but we can find little ways in which we can bless others just as God has blessed us and start from there.

Exercise 5.2

How have you been generous lately? How's that charitable living going?

---

[81] St Matthew xix.16-30

Lust versus Chastity and Continence

Properly speaking, Lust is an unbridled and uncontrolled passion that infects our consciousness. We perceive it markedly in the lust for sex, but it also seeks a complete possession of the people we desire. We can have a lust for power just as much as a lust for sex. Whenever we indulge those thoughts about controlling another person's actions like a puppet, we are committing Lust. Whenever we are consumed with a burning fire to possess, we are committing Lust.

It is different from Envy as we shall see, but you can get an idea for how Lust is more generally interpreted when you see shoppers pressed up against doors of a department store waiting for the doors to open. You can see how this related with the Lust we have for human beings, especially sexual Lust.

When we are in the fires of Lust, we forget important things – usually the health and happiness of other people. The shoppers lusting after a bargain are oblivious to the people they are trampling underfoot and to the harried sales clerks who are trying to deal with their demands. The businessman lusting after control of a company is oblivious to the people whose lives he is ruining on his rise to the top. The man lusting after a stripper forgets that she has resorted to such an awful and miserable activity because she is addicted to drugs, or is simply trying to make ends meet, or is even trying to appease the man abusing her to do this in the first place. Lust doesn't care about others! It is pure selfish desire.

St Paul says to St Timothy, "Flee also youthful lusts: but follow righteousness, faith, charity, peace, with them that call on the Lord out of a pure heart."[82]

The way to combat Lust is by Continence. We contain our desires by remembering other people and their lives. The physical make-up of our bodies means that we do have sexual attractions and this is how we are meant to be. We may get these thoughts, but we don't have to entertain them. We need to contain the fire by reminding it of its limits and stepping back from the heat. When we see that a bargain is nothing more than a thing and less valuable than any human being could be, then we are containing our desire. Likewise, when we see an attractive person, we thank God for their beauty and pray to Him that their lives may be full of happiness, and that their troubles in life may cease.

The combatting of sexual lust is with Chastity in which we remain faithful to our marital state. Even if we are single, then we still cannot lust after someone without committing adultery. If we are married, we can lust after our spouse if we seek to control them without any thought for their person. Chastity bids us avoid situations in which we might be tempted to think of someone in a way that diminishes their humanity. In marriage, we are faithful to our spouse if we play our part in our relationship with them and give ourselves to their good. In the single state, we must remain celibate until we have found that person to whom we want to commit our lives.

The Sin of Lust is a particularly difficult sin to overcome given that it appears in so many ways. However, by stepping back, thinking more widely about the situation, and praying to God, it can be overcome.

---

[82] II Timothy ii.22

Exercise 5.3

Think about your lusts. Can you step back from them?

Sloth versus Diligence

In Sloth, we find the desire not to make any contribution to the world. We seek only to maintain our own comfort at the expense of the needs of those around us. We do not wish to lift a finger because the matter of other people being human doesn't matter. Sloth is very similar to saying that there is no point to doing things. When we suffer from Sloth, we are not just being lazy, we are actively saying that nothing in the world has any point, and so we maintain a comfortable life for ourselves to sit and wait it out.

The ancient Church Fathers saw in Sloth a spiritual sadness, a despair that makes religious duty a chore and not a joy.[83] Of course, saying our prayers can seem tedious at times, especially if we've become over-familiar with the words through repeated prayer.

Sloth prevents us from doing good things in the world, even if those good things are seemingly insignificant, ignored, or derided. Sloth says we should worship nothing, save perhaps our own comfortable numbness in the darkness of an irredeemable world.

Yet, look! The Christian Faith says that there is always hope. It says that there are things worth caring about – indeed, the thing we should be caring about most is what God thinks. The most seemingly insignificant task well-performed is probably of

---

[83] E.g. St John Cassian *Institutes* Book X

greater joy to God than any prize the world might give us for a great work of art, of writing, or of self-sacrifice.

St Paul says, "whatsoever ye do, do it heartily, as to the Lord, and not unto men".[84]

The cure for Sloth is Diligence – taking care to do everything for the love of God – brushing your teeth, saving a butterfly from a spider's web, smiling at a stranger. Remember that God can act through you, and that through your good deeds, you will be bringing more good into the world which will bring light to others in darkness. Your merits, even little tiny ones, count and ripple through Time and Space.

Depression is certainly something that affects so many people these days. Sometimes that is clinical; sometimes that is due to horrible things happening around us, or on the news. However we feel, we still must look for ways to bring the blessing of God into a dark world. Diligence is hard work, but it is good work and pays dividends by making such a difference to the lives of others and thus to ourselves.

Exercise 5.4
What depresses you most? Find and read the words to the anthem O Thou the Central Orb. If you can listen to the music by Charles Wood or Orlando Gibbons too, do so. What do you hear in those words? How can you turn that depression around?

Pride and Vanity versus Humility

Just as Sloth is formed in being comfortable with our identity, pride and vanity seek only to dress up our view of ourselves. Vanity is the sin of elevating ourselves with empty importance, and pride is the belief that our presence is more supreme than

---

[84] Colossian iii.23

those around us. In seeing ourselves as the most important aspect of our lives, we find only ourselves to worship. This is the great sin that traditionally threw Lucifer out of Heaven to become the one we know as the Devil. We'll look at him later!

It is okay to take pride in what we do, or in our appearance provided that these aren't the object of our attention. As we said above, doing something little well for God is so much better than doing something enormous just in order to receive praise from other people. Jesus says a lot of hard things against the religious leaders of His day who revelled in being seen to be important.

In the fourteenth chapter of St Luke's Gospel, we read:

> [Jesus] put forth a parable to those [Pharisees and Chief Priests] which were bidden, when He marked how they chose out the chief rooms; saying unto them, When thou art bidden of any man to a wedding, sit not down in the highest room; lest a more honourable man than thou be bidden of him; And he that bade thee and him come and say to thee, Give this man place; and thou begin with shame to take the lowest room. But when thou art bidden, go and sit down in the lowest room; that when he that bade thee cometh, he may say unto thee, Friend, go up higher: then shalt thou have worship in the presence of them that sit at meat with thee. For whosoever exalteth himself shall be abased; and he that humbleth himself shall be exalted.[85]

The cure for Pride and Vanity is Humility, but people often get the wrong end of the stick when they think about that. Humility is not doing yourself down. It is not saying that you are the lowest of the low. Humility is a real, honest appraisal of yourself and

---

[85] St Luke xiv.7-11

your work. Humility is about being down-to-earth. Indeed, the word "humility" has the same root as "human" and this root means "of the earth." We can think back to Adam being made by God out of the dust of the Earth. Human is what we are, no more, no less. Humility, then, is about seeing ourselves as we really are, and asking God for the grace to do so.

Much has been written by the saints about Humility, especially by St Benedict.[86] We need to remember that we are as human as everyone else and that the qualities that we value in us are gifts from God. We need to learn to value the gifts of others and learn to see God's image in them. The more we love others properly, the less pride that we will have. The more that we learn to see God's values, the less importance we will give to things that really are insignificant.

Exercise 5.5
How down to earth are you? In what ways do you compare yourself with other people? How will you learn humility?

Wrath versus Patience

In Wrath, we seek to impress our own justice upon others in revenge for an injustice perceived against us. Note that, in wrath, again we seek to impress our identity on the world around – in this case, our own sense of justice regardless of whether that justice is indeed really just and fair! This is the point, in order to bring people to justice we need complete knowledge of the situation. We can certainly be angry, but when we are angry we must recognise that it is only a feeling and not permission to seek payment or revenge.

---

[86] St Benedict *The Rule* Chapter VII

St Paul says, "Dearly beloved, avenge not yourselves, but rather give place unto wrath: for it is written, Vengeance is mine; I will repay, saith the Lord." [87]

We have to worship God in His Goodness and trust Him when it comes to bringing people and situations to true justice. This isn't easy, especially as there are so many miscarriages of justice around us. But we must also realise that there is very little point in being angry with things we cannot control. If our party doesn't win the General Election, then we can be angry that the opposition have won, but this doesn't solve anything until the next General Election.

The cure for Wrath is Patience. You may have heard the old phrase "count to ten" when you're angry. The practice is very helpful: we need to distance ourselves from our feelings of anger so that we can see the wider picture. For the most part, we just need to put up with things as they are until a Christian solution presents itself. Patience really means the ability to suffer well. There is an old tradition called "offering it up" which means that when we are in a situation where we are angry and tempted to sin, we offer up the situation to God as a sacrifice for others in the same situation. Remember that Love is all about making things holy, willing the Good for others, no matter what it cost us. As members of the Church and its priesthood, it is perfectly within our right to make sacrifices of our troubles for the good of the world, and we should learn to do this well. This gives our personal suffering a purpose for a greater glory of God and for our closer relationship with Him.

---

[87] Romans xii.19

Of course, the suffering of other people can make us angry. While that anger may goad us into a good action, we must always pray to God that we may work humbly in His Name and not in our own sense of justice and right which may not be the same as His.

Exercise 5.6
What makes you angry? How can you offer the situation up to God?

Envy versus Kindness

Envy really is the saddest sin: it is a desire to possess that which another has and we have not. Here there is always that fear of missing out, of entitlement, of seeing those who we want to be and wanting to be them to their detriment and to our benefit. While some sinful pleasure (however fleeting) can be gained from Gluttony and Lust, Envy has no pleasure in it at all, just grudging and ill-will. The Ten Commandments tell us specifically not to covet, and so they are commandment directly against Envy. It is clear that Envy is destructive and must be cut out of our lives quickly.

In the Proverbs, we read, "A sound heart is the life of the flesh: but envy the rottenness of the bones."[88] St James tells us, "But if ye have bitter envying and strife in your hearts, glory not, and lie not against the truth. This wisdom descendeth not from above, but is earthly, sensual, devilish. For where envying and strife is, there is confusion and every evil work."[89]

If we envy what someone else has, then we miss out on what God has in store for us. God wants us to live our own lives, not someone else's. We know that we should detach our concern from

---

[88] Proverbs xiv.30
[89] James iii.13-14

our possessions so that we can love God, so envy can't take place there.

The cure for Envy is simple kindness. We need to rejoice in the fortune of others as well as bewail the misfortune of others. We need to see their lives as beautifully different from our own, and to regard ourselves as beloved children of God in our own right. If we covet someone's house, we need to ask ourselves why, and isolate what the real desire is. It may be that what we really want is very different from what we think we want. Again we must pray to God to show us what we need rather than what we want.

We need to learn to enjoy other people as they are, and rejoice in doing good things for them, building up a community rather than letting envy rot us from within.

Exercise 5.7

If you envy someone, try and find out what it is you really want, and ask God to supply that, rather than what you think you want. Then find a way of being kind to the person whom you envy.

But Remember!

It is all very much a good thing to recognise Sin in our lives, and knowing our weaknesses, but if we allow the process of self-examination happen without God's light, then we can easily convince ourselves that we are wrong, corrupt and thoroughly evil. Certainly evil things do happen at our hands whether we want them or not, but we are still the creation of God. We are here because God wants us to be, and He wants us to be with Him. We see the lengths that He goes to in order to bring us back to Him. The answers to why evil things happen to good people, and why even the best people do evil things do not lie in a text book: they lie in the Cross of Christ.

There is one unforgivable sin and that is a complete rejection of God.[90] If you worry that you've committed the unforgivable sin, then don't worry! – you haven't! Worrying that you've sinned shows that you care about what God wants for you, and that there are the seeds of repentance within you. Repent of the sins you have committed, forgive others, and be reconciled with Christ. Whatever wrong you have done will be washed away. God really does promise that!

God says to us through the prophet Isaiah, "Come now, and let us reason together, saith the LORD: though your sins be as scarlet, they shall be as white as snow; though they be red like crimson, they shall be as wool."[91]

God's wish is the destruction of sin, not the destruction of us. We can be the authors of our own destruction, but God will not be.

St John says:

> if any man sin, we have an advocate with the Father, Jesus Christ the righteous: And he is the propitiation for our sins: and not for ours only, but also for the sins of the whole world. And hereby we do know that we know him, if we keep his commandments.[92]

This is why the Gospel of Our Lord truly is good news!

Exercise 5.8
When next you feel discouraged by your sins, find a crucifix and see the lengths to which God goes in order to keep you with Him.

---

[90] St Matthew xii.31
[91] Isaiah i.18
[92] I John ii.1-3

There is nothing you can do to change the fact that you are loved so much!

Chapter 6: What does the Church offer me?

Grace

You will by now have seen that the Church is THE community of Christians built up by God to be a blessing to the world. The Church has a Mission to bring the love of God to people and to bring them back into the fullness of a relationship with God through the Incarnation of Our Lord Jesus Christ. Yet, Christians are not perfect and there have been horrible atrocities committed in God's name. This emphasises the need to trust God and keep faith even when He seems distant.

However, the Church does offer something wonderful. Since she is built by God, the Church offers nothing less than the active presence of God Himself. This is what we mean by Grace – God's active presence that everyone can experience in faith. Grace is God's gift to the Church to give to all humanity. Indeed, the Church herself is a gift of grace to humanity: she offers an experience of God's active presence.

Exercise 6.1

Have you experienced God's active presence? How did you know it was God? How was it active for you?

We call a way that God gives grace to His people a sacrament: the Orthodox Church calls them Mysteries because they open the way to an unfathomable relationship with God. Traditionally, the Church has recognised seven sacraments, though there has been no official statement that limits the number of sacraments to seven within the Primitive Church. However, the Church certainly has God's authority to give people His grace through seven sacraments. In the first chapter of his Gospel, St John says of Jesus that "of His fulness have all we received, and grace for grace. For the law was given by Moses, but grace and truth came by Jesus Christ."[93] This means that the Church has truly received God in the person of Our Lord Jesus Christ, and that she has received grace to give grace, i.e. God wants the Church to distribute His grace through sacraments.

A sacrament does something: it has a purpose and a prescribed means of doing it, and nothing can change that because it has been instituted by Christ Himself. If an established sacrament can change, then that change ceases to be part of the Catholic Church because the Church exists for all people in Time in the same way.

We will now look at each of the seven sacraments that God has given the Church and see what they mean for each of us.

Baptism

We have already looked a little at Baptism and its relationship with Sin in the Nicene Creed. Baptism was indeed instituted as a means of grace by Christ.

Exercise 6.2

Read the third chapter of St Matthew's Gospel.[94] *How does Jesus change St John the Baptist's baptism?*

St Paul says that, as Jesus was baptised to identify Himself with us, "Therefore we are buried with him by baptism into death: that like as Christ was raised up from the dead by the glory of the Father, even so we also should walk in newness of life."[95]

---

[93] St John i.16-17
[94] St Matthew iii
[95] Romans vi.4

Baptism rids us of the sin that we had before we were baptised, and opens us to being able to receive the other sacraments which are open to God's people. In some sense, not only does it cure the sins that we have committed, but it also inoculates us against the sins that we commit after Baptism by allowing us to receive the absolution that God has given the Church through which He pronounces His forgiveness.

Baptism is the means by which we become full members of the Church, see the quote from St Paul's letter to the Colossians when we were discussing the phrase "I acknowledge one baptism for sins."[96]

We know that Christ wants us to Baptise, and that Baptism has a clear purpose. It also has to be done in the right way. In the twenty-eighth chapter of the Gospel of St Matthew, we read:

> And Jesus came and spake unto them, saying, All power is given unto me in heaven and in earth. Go ye therefore, and teach all nations, baptizing them in the name of the Father, and of the Son, and of the Holy Ghost: Teaching them to observe all things whatsoever I have commanded you: and, lo, I am with you alway, even unto the end of the world. Amen.[97]

When the Church baptises, the priest immerses the person (or pours water over them) three times in the name of the Father, Son and Holy Ghost. No other way of doing so is valid. In Baptism, Christ brings that person fully into membership with Him.

We see, therefore, that Baptism gives us the active presence of God to become a member of His body through the action that

---

[96] Colossians ii.8-13
[97] St Matthew xxviii.18-20

Jesus has shown us. This means that Baptism is a sacrament – indeed it is our first sacrament that we receive as a Christian!

The Mass

We have discussed the Mass a little earlier, too. It is also known as the Eucharist or Holy Communion, and it is a central element of Christian Worship. In St Matthew's Gospel, we read:

> And as they were eating, Jesus took bread, and blessed it, and brake it, and gave it to the disciples, and said, Take, eat; this is my body. And he took the cup, and gave thanks, and gave it to them, saying, Drink ye all of it; For this is my blood of the new testament, which is shed for many for the remission of sins.[98]

In St Luke's Gospel, we read:

> And he took bread, and gave thanks, and brake it, and gave unto them, saying, This is my body which is given for you: this do in remembrance of me. Likewise also the cup after supper, saying, This cup is the new testament in my blood, which is shed for you.[99]

We can see from these accounts that this is not only something that Jesus has instituted, but something that He wants us to do in remembrance of Him. But why?

St Paul says, "The cup of blessing which we bless, is it not the communion of the blood of Christ? The bread which we break, is it not the communion of the body of Christ?"[100]

---

[98] St Matthew xxvi.26-28
[99] St Luke xxii.19-20
[100] I Corinthians x.16

Exercise 6.3

Read the sixth chapter of St John's Gospel.[101] What does Jesus say about His Body and Blood? Why does He use the word "indeed" in the fifty-fifth verse?

In the Anglican Catholic Church, we believe strongly that the bread and wine at Mass really become the Body and Blood of Christ when they are consecrated – we call this the Real Presence of Christ. They may look the same if we look with the eyes of disbelief but, when we have prayed the liturgy and trust in the words of Our Lord, then the Bread and Wine are replaced with the Body and Blood of Christ. We don't ask how that change works because ultimately only God understands what is truly real, but rather allow ourselves to embrace the reality of Christ within us when we eat His body and drink His blood. This is not cannibalism which is the eating of dead flesh, but we are taking into ourselves the whole living body of Christ.

There used to be a slogan, "you are what you eat" and this is very true of the Mass, for this is the process by which we become closer to God. In the Old Testament, the flesh of the animal offered in sacrifice for the forgiveness of sins was consumed by the person offering it.[102] It is clear that Jesus offers Himself as a sacrifice on the altar of the Cross. In the letter to the Hebrews, we read:

> For Christ is not entered into the holy places made with hands, which are the figures of the true; but into heaven itself, now to appear in the presence of God for us: Nor yet that he should offer himself often, as the high priest entereth into the holy place every year with blood of others; For then must he often have suffered since the foundation of the world: but now once in the end of the world hath he appeared to put away sin by the sacrifice

---

[101] St John vi, especially St John vi.55
[102] Leviticus vi.24-30

of himself. And as it is appointed unto men once to die, but after this the judgment: So Christ was once offered to bear the sins of many; and unto them that look for him shall he appear the second time without sin unto salvation.[103]

The Mass, then, is a sacrifice instituted by Jesus Himself as both priest and the victim. Its purpose is for the forgiveness of sins, the reconciliation of human beings with God, and the feeding of each Christian with the substance of God so that we can become like Him. The priest is to follow the formula set out above. He takes bread and wine and repeats the words of Jesus. This is why the Mass is a sacrament.

When Jesus says, "do this in remembrance of me," the word "remembrance" is something stronger than just "remember." Rather we deliberately putting ourselves back into that time and place. It really is an effort of will and intention. So, we get a notion of just how deep this sacrament is as a Mystery. Christ only ever offered Himself once upon the Cross. That means that we are not crucifying Him again and again every time we say Mass. Rather, at every Mass we are brought into Communion with God and the Church. The sacrifice of every Mass is that same sacrifice offered by Jesus at His Last Supper. In the Mass we become part of that same Last Supper, and therefore we are linked to every celebration of the Mass throughout History! This is very deep, but very wonderful! It is why Anglican Catholics take the Mass very seriously indeed! Every Christian needs to receive Communion at least once a year, but it is a good thing to receive it regularly!

The Mass is called the Eucharist because, in our sacrifice of the Mass, we also offer a sacrifice of thanksgiving which is what the

---

[103] Hebrews ix.24-28

word Eucharist means. When we leave the Mass, we are sent out (the Latin for "sent" is *missus* from which we get the word Mass) with renewed vigour to do our work as a Christian. Both the Baptism and Eucharist are sacraments that every Christian should receive in their lifetime. Through them, they bring the means to Salvation by reconciling us to God in Jesus Christ.

Confirmation

It is all very well that Christians become part of the Church, but they still need to work for and with the Church in their daily lives. Each one of us has a mission, a vocation by God to work His will in the world in a way that is in keeping with who we are. In order to do the work of God, we need to fan into flame the fire of the Holy Ghost Who has dwelt within us since our Baptism. The presence of the Holy Ghost is ignited within us like a pilot light when we are baptised with water and the Spirit. In order for us to do God's work, we have to allow the Holy Spirit to burn in us, to breathe through us. Just as the flesh of Our Lord Jesus Christ ultimately makes us like God, so the Holy Ghost working in us allows us to breathe like Him, too.

In the eighth chapter of Acts we read that people in Samaria were becoming Christian. So the Church sent to Samaria Peter and John,

> Who, when they were come down, prayed for them, that they might receive the Holy Ghost: (For as yet he was fallen upon none of them: only they were baptized in the name of the Lord Jesus.) Then laid they their hands on them, and they received the Holy Ghost.[104]

This is the sacrament of Confirmation. Our capacity to receive the Holy Ghost is strengthened by the laying on of hands by a bishop

---

[104] Acts viii.15-17

who says, "receive the Holy Ghost". For an adult who is coming to Baptism, Confirmation often happens soon afterwards.

It is not necessary that a Christian be confirmed, but it is encouraged because it consecrates your life of work for the Church. Many tasks that the Church needs to do requires people who are confirmed precisely because they have that seal of the Holy Ghost in their lives. St John says, "the anointing which ye have received of Him abideth in you, and ye need not that any man teach you: but as the same anointing teacheth you of all things, and is truth, and is no lie, and even as it hath taught you, ye shall abide in Him".[105] The anointing he is talking about is precisely confirmation with the Holy Ghost.

Confirmation gives an active presence of God through the Holy Ghost as a resource to tap when we are needing refreshment. Jesus says, "whosoever drinketh of the water that I shall give him shall never thirst; but the water that I shall give him shall be in him a well of water springing up into everlasting life".[106] The water that He is referring to is the Holy Ghost Who will refresh us when we need it.

Exercise 6.4

Read the fourth chapter of St John's Gospel in full.[107] *How do you see the role of the Holy Ghost in this conversation between Jesus and the Canaanite woman?*

Confession

The sad fact is that we sin, and the vast majority of us will sin after we are baptised probably more than we did before we are

---

[105] I John ii.27
[106] St John iv.14
[107] St John iv.

baptised – that's fallen humanity for you! As we have discovered, every single sin separates us from God, and therefore we need to repent of every single sin so that we can return to God. To this end, Jesus has given the Church authority to forgive sins. In the twentieth chapter of St John's Gospel, we read that after Jesus' resurrection, He appeared to His disciples and

> ...breathed on them, and saith unto them, Receive ye the Holy Ghost: Whose soever sins ye remit, they are remitted unto them; and whose soever sins ye retain, they are retained.[108]

From Jesus' very words, through the priests and bishops, the Church can forgive sins in Jesus' Name if we truly repent. St John says, "If we say that we have no sin, we deceive ourselves, and the truth is not in us. If we confess our sins, [God] is faithful and just to forgive us our sins, and to cleanse us from all unrighteousness."[109] In this way, we have a way of confessing our sins to God and finding forgiveness.

The Sacrament of Confession is open to anyone who is Baptised, and who feels that they need assurance of God's forgiveness. You can go to a priest and confess your sins and, through that priest, Jesus Himself will forgive you your sins and offer support and advice. Of course, the Church recognises that confessing your sins is a very difficult and private thing. To make it easier for you, every priest who hears confession makes a solemn oath never, ever to reveal or even act on anything said in that confession. If he does, he will effectively be thrown out of the Church! You will see that this is a very serious punishment for a priest! The vast majority of priests, however, will be willing to hear your confession properly and keep everything a strict secret for your benefit out of their loving duty to you as a Christian. At the end of

---

[108] St John xx.22-23
[109] I John i.8-9

your confession, the priest will say, "Our Lord Jesus Christ, who hath left power to his Church to absolve all sinners who truly repent and believe in him, of his great mercy forgive thee thine offences: And by his authority committed to me, I absolve thee from all thy sins, In the Name of the Father, and of the Son, and of the Holy Ghost. Amen."

We should really aim to go to confession once a year in order to unburden ourselves of sins, but the Anglican Catholic Church adopts the policy that Confession is not something to be legislated or demanded of its members, but rather encouraged and left to the conscience of the individual. Archbishop Michael Ramsay once said on the topic of whether you should go to confession, "all may, none must, some should".

The active presence of God is there to forgive sins confessed, and the words of the priest pronouncing absolution make Confession a sacrament.

Exercise 6.5
Does anything worry you about the sacrament of Confession? If so, think about how seriously a priest must take it. Might you want to try it for yourself?

Holy Matrimony

According to St John, Jesus' first miracle took place at a wedding in Cana.[110] In providing this miracle, Jesus consecrates the whole idea of marriage. In our society, Marriage is seen as a legal contract, but the Church views marriage as a sacrament and therefore more strongly than just words on a piece of paper.

---

[110] St John ii.1-11

On the topic of marriage, Jesus quotes Genesis, "Therefore shall a man leave his father and his mother, and shall cleave unto his wife: and they shall be one flesh."[111] Essentially, a marriage creates an inseparable union between a husband and wife. Since God is our Creator, only He can make one flesh out of husband and wife. In the Anglican Catholic Church, we believe that there is no such thing as divorce, for Jesus says, "What therefore God hath joined together, let not man put asunder... Whosoever shall put away his wife, and marry another, committeth adultery against her. And if a woman shall put away her husband, and be married to another, she committeth adultery."[112]

This talk of divorce may seem very negative, but the point is that, in a marriage, God Himself is present joining husband and wife together inseparably – this is a wonderful thing! We therefore see that marriage gives the married couple grace to be together forever, and that, when difficulties in marriage do arise, there will be support by the Church and, more importantly, by the Holy Ghost to assist the couple through them so that they come out all the stronger together. This is an important point: it is the couple getting married who are the ministers of the sacrament: the priest at a wedding serves to represent God, bestow His blessing on the marriage and to demonstrate His presence in all marriages.

Exercise 6.6
The Catholic Church does not recognise same-sex marriage as being a real sacramental marriage. Why do you think that is?

Extreme Unction
What happens when we get sick, or even approach Death? As Christians, we do have a duty to all those who are sick or dying. Jesus bids us look after the sick, praying with them and

---

[111] Genesis ii.24, St Matthew xix.5
[112] St Matthew xix.6,9

ministering to them. In the ninth chapter of St Luke's Gospel, we read,

> Then He called his twelve disciples together, and gave them power and authority over all devils, and to cure diseases. And He sent them to preach the kingdom of God, and to heal the sick. And He said unto them, Take nothing for your journey, neither staves, nor scrip, neither bread, neither money; neither have two coats apiece. And whatsoever house ye enter into, there abide, and thence depart. And whosoever will not receive you, when ye go out of that city, shake off the very dust from your feet for a testimony against them. And they departed, and went through the towns, preaching the gospel, and healing every where.[113]

It is clear that Jesus has set up a pattern for ministering to the sick. While the Church does not cure diseases in the medical way, it does help with the spiritual effects of those diseases by bringing hope to those in distress and supporting them in their troubles. However, if everyone has sufficient faith and it is in keeping with the will of God, there is always the possibility of a miraculous healing. They still happen today!

St James says,

> Is any sick among you? let him call for the elders of the church; and let them pray over him, anointing him with oil in the name of the Lord: And the prayer of faith shall save the sick, and the Lord shall raise him up; and if he have committed sins, they shall be forgiven him.[114]

---

[113] St Luke ix.1-6
[114] James v.14-15

Notice that the Church is told to anoint the sick with oil. Just as fire, and water are symbols of the Holy Ghost, so is oil. It is for those in danger of death that the Church has been given a particular sacrament to help them on their way. This is called Extreme Unction and it is used for all people in danger of death. The person is anointed with oil by a priest so that the presence of the Holy Ghost can be with them and, if they should die, bring them through death into Eternal Life.

Exercise 6.7

Think about your own death and what you would need in order to die well, without fear, and without worry. Then give those thoughts to God and relax in the knowledge that He will bring you through your death.

Holy Orders

You will notice that all the sacraments above are performed by a Bishop or a Priest. In fact, with the permission of a priest, a deacon may also baptise. Bishops, priests and deacons form the clergy of the Church. They are still laymen, just like any other Christian, but God has separated them out for special duties, in particular in administering the sacraments and witnessing marriages as a representative of God's presence. Where do the clergy come from? The answer is another sacrament called Ordination. We are told in the third chapter of St Mark's Gospel that Jesus "ordained twelve, that they should be with him, and that he might send them forth to preach, and to have power to heal sicknesses, and to cast out devils:"[115] The original Twelve Apostles were the first Bishops of the Church. This included Judas who later betrayed Jesus and handed him over to the Jewish authorities who crucified Him. Of course, afterwards, Judas went and hanged himself, and something very unpleasant

---

[115] St Mark iii.14-15

happened to his body. After Judas' death, we are told in the first chapter of the Book of Acts,

> Peter stood up in the midst of the disciples, and said, (the number of names together were about an hundred and twenty,) Men and brethren, this scripture must needs have been fulfilled, which the Holy Ghost by the mouth of David spake before concerning Judas, which was guide to them that took Jesus. For he was numbered with us, and had obtained part of this ministry... For it is written in the book of Psalms, Let his habitation be desolate, and let no man dwell therein: and his bishoprick let another take. Wherefore of these men which have companied with us all the time that the Lord Jesus went in and out among us, Beginning from the baptism of John, unto that same day that he was taken up from us, must one be ordained to be a witness with us of his resurrection. And they appointed two, Joseph called Barsabas, who was surnamed Justus, and Matthias. And they prayed, and said, Thou, Lord, which knowest the hearts of all men, shew whether of these two thou hast chosen, That he may take part of this ministry and apostleship, from which Judas by transgression fell, that he might go to his own place. And they gave forth their lots; and the lot fell upon Matthias; and he was numbered with the eleven apostles.[116]

Here we see the appointment of the first new Bishop, St Matthias.

Exercise 6.8

What happens in the second chapter of the Book of Acts?[117]

---

[116] Acts i.15-26
[117] Acts ii

These original Twelve Apostles and their successors are the Bishops of the Catholic Church. Every Bishop in the Church today is a successor to the Apostles and an inheritor of their authority given to them by Jesus. They were not alone. In the sixth chapter of Acts, we read

> And in those days, when the number of the disciples was multiplied, there arose a murmuring of the Grecians against the Hebrews, because their widows were neglected in the daily ministration. Then the twelve called the multitude of the disciples unto them, and said, It is not reason that we should leave the word of God, and serve tables. Wherefore, brethren, look ye out among you seven men of honest report, full of the Holy Ghost and wisdom, whom we may appoint over this business. But we will give ourselves continually to prayer, and to the ministry of the word. And the saying pleased the whole multitude: and they chose Stephen, a man full of faith and of the Holy Ghost, and Philip, and Prochorus, and Nicanor, and Timon, and Parmenas, and Nicolas a proselyte of Antioch: Whom they set before the apostles: and when they had prayed, they laid their hands on them.[118]

These seven men became the first deacons – assistants to Bishops. You notice that the Bishops laid their hands on these first deacons. This is something that is common to all ordinations. St Paul says to St Timothy "Neglect not the gift that is in thee, which was given thee by prophecy, with the laying on of the hands of the presbytery." The presbytery is the group of priests ordained to represent the Bishop and assist him in sacramental duties.

---

[118] Acts vi.1-6

St Paul also tells St Timothy about the qualities of bishops and deacons.

> This is a true saying, If a man desire the office of a bishop, he desireth a good work. A bishop then must be blameless, the husband of one wife, vigilant, sober, of good behaviour, given to hospitality, apt to teach; Not given to wine, no striker, not greedy of filthy lucre; but patient, not a brawler, not covetous; One that ruleth well his own house, having his children in subjection with all gravity; (For if a man know not how to rule his own house, how shall he take care of the church of God?) Not a novice, lest being lifted up with pride he fall into the condemnation of the devil. Moreover he must have a good report of them which are without; lest he fall into reproach and the snare of the devil. Likewise must the deacons be grave, not doubletongued, not given to much wine, not greedy of filthy lucre; Holding the mystery of the faith in a pure conscience. And let these also first be proved; then let them use the office of a deacon, being found blameless. Even so must their wives be grave, not slanderers, sober, faithful in all things. Let the deacons be the husbands of one wife, ruling their children and their own houses well. For they that have used the office of a deacon well purchase to themselves a good degree, and great boldness in the faith which is in Christ Jesus.[119]

Not everyone is called to be a bishop, priest or deacon. The duties of the clergy are to ensure that they perform the sacraments properly. They are to be ordained properly so that they can receive the same authority to perform the sacraments from Jesus. You will note that the clergy are all male, and the Catholic Church

---

[119] I Timothy iii.1-13

does not have authority to ordain women. This is because, despite including women as an integral part of the Church rather than letting them be by-standers as did the leaders of the day, Jesus only chooses men to be the first bishops and thus represent Him at the altar. This is not to make women inferior to men otherwise He would not have chosen them to be the first witnesses of His resurrection. [120] It is a recognition that God made men and women to be different, and to rejoice in their differences, just as Christ rejoices in the Church and the Church rejoices in Him. We have to be obedient to God if we want to love Him, even if what He says challenges our ideas of equality.

Any bishop who does try to ordain a woman ceases to be a member of the Catholic Church, as does the woman, for the simple reason that neither of them are being Catholic – they are changing the terms on which Jesus gives us the assurance of His grace. This is why the Catholic Church cannot be in communion with Churches that ordain women, though we do recognise that their intention is to follow Christ.

At an ordination, God is actively present to instil His authority by the laying on of hands by a bishop. A bishop can preside at all seven sacraments. A priest may only say Mass, Baptise, Marry, give Extreme Unction, and Absolve. A deacon may only baptise with the priest's permission, but assists the priest and bishop in the sacraments.

These seven sacraments are how the Church is able to support its members through God's grace. There are many other ways that the Church can support people, and it is important to realise that not every way of ministering to people requires Ordination. Everyone has something that they can do to build up the church,

---

[120] St Matthew xxviii.1, St John xx

and it is a matter of listening and talking to discover what your vocation is.

Chapter 7: What does the world get wrong?

Now that we have looked at what Christians believe, how they live and how they pray, we need to look at a few topics that follow from these. Many of these ideas have been misunderstood by people and these misunderstandings have made it into popular culture and are used as sticks to beat the Church. It is important that we know the truth so that we do not fall into error and find ourselves in dangerous territory.

Life after Death?

Let us be clear from the outset. No-one knows for sure what happens after we die except God. Our Lord Jesus has made us promises about what goes on and has shown us something of what lies beyond Death, but we have to trust His word and the testimony of Holy Scripture. We know that faith is the substance of things hoped for, the evidence of things not seen.[121] It is not scientific evidence, but the evidence within us. All we can do is trust and believe what Jesus says about what happens when we die.

And what does He say?

If we read His parables carefully, we can understand that He is talking in analogy. There is a wedding feast in which a bridegroom arrives suddenly, welcoming into his wedding-feast the wise virgins who have kept oil in their lamps ready, but shutting out those who have wasted their oil.[122] There is a parable of weeds growing in a field of wheat which, when harvest comes are thrown into the fire.[123] There are others as well. We have

---

[121] Hebrews xi.1
[122] St Matthew xxv.1-13
[123] St Matthew xiii.24-30

already said that we believe in the Resurrection of the Dead, but it is clear that there is to be some separation after death of those who accept God and those who reject Him.

The Book of Revelation shows the downfall of Evil, shut away into a fiery pit which we call Hell.[124] It also shows the New Jerusalem as a place where the Church will live with God for Eternity.[125] It's also clear that we do not turn into angels when we die, but rather, when we are resurrected, we receive our bodies again. What is meant by Heaven is this state of Eternity with God.

It is also clear that all sin separates us from God. Does that mean that if we die in sin, we cannot go to Heaven? That would seem to be unfair. Yet it is also unfair that someone who commits suicide just to avoid the penalties of judgement on earth should get away scot-free. Only God will judge on these matters, but it is clear that His judgement is literally the putting right of everything that is wrong.

St Paul says:

> According to the grace of God which is given unto me, as a wise masterbuilder, I have laid the foundation, and another buildeth thereon. But let every man take heed how he buildeth thereupon. For other foundation can no man lay than that is laid, which is Jesus Christ. Now if any man build upon this foundation gold, silver, precious stones, wood, hay, stubble; Every man's work shall be made manifest: for the day shall declare it, because it shall be revealed by fire; and the fire shall try every man's work of what sort it is. If any man's work abide which he hath built thereupon, he shall receive a

---

[124] Revelation xx
[125] Revelation xxi

reward. If any man's work shall be burned, he shall suffer loss: but he himself shall be saved; yet so as by fire.[126]

It seems that there is justice beyond Death which will perfect us and bring us to God. However, those who reject God and refuse to repent of their sin cannot be with God because where God is, there can be no sin, and vice versa.

The concept of Hell as a fiery pit seems frightening to us. We get the idea of an Eternal punishment for our sins, that God punishes us eternally for sins that we committed in Time. This is not quite true. We have a choice to repent of our sins, or not. If we do, then we can return to God. If not, then we must stay away from Him. In short, we literally choose to go to Hell if we refuse to repent of our sins. This is a punishment only in the sense of people cutting off their nose to spite their face, but refusing to acknowledge the truth when face to face with God.

Medieval depictions of Hell do somewhat exaggerate the situation. A better description of it might be found in C.S.Lewis' book, *The Great Divorce*, in which Hell is a continued life of misery without light, without warmth, filled with utter sadness. The Lake of Fire is an analogy to the vitality of the glorious human spirit created by God trying to live without God and thus having a burning hunger for something the very thing that it always refuses and can now never know.

Exercise 7.1
Read the twenty-fifth chapter of St Matthew's Gospel.[127] What does it say about our fate?

---

[126] I Corinthians iii.10-15
[127] St Matthew xxv

Interestingly, the fires of Hell may be everlasting, but does that mean that those who go there stay eternally? Surprisingly, things aren't cut and dried on that. There are those Christians who believe that a stay in Hell is eternal just as a stay in Heaven is eternal. There are those who say it is not. Yet, one thing is clear, the Christian should not be motivated by a fear of Hell unless it is a fear of being separated from God.

We should be motivated by the love of God which we have grown and cultivated over our lifetimes. We should rather seek to be transformed by God, even if that transformation is painful, so that we can find Him at last and be with Him on His terms.

St John says, "Beloved, now are we the sons of God, and it doth not yet appear what we shall be: but we know that, when He shall appear, we shall be like Him; for we shall see him as He is."[128] This is God's promise to us. This is true Heaven and it goes beyond our understanding. All we can gather from the twenty-first chapter of the Book of Revelation is that it will be like the life we know now, only better, fuller, and that we shall be like God.

Exercise 7.2

If you're worried about Hell, then think on what St Paul says. "Finally, brethren, whatsoever things are true, whatsoever things are honest, whatsoever things are just, whatsoever things are pure, whatsoever things are lovely, whatsoever things are of good report; if there be any virtue, and if there be any praise, think on these things."[129] Spend a moment of your time each day doing just that.

---

[128] I John iii.2
[129] Philippians iv.8

Mary, Queen of Heaven

Many people seem to have a bit of a problem with the Virgin Mary, that Catholics worship her instead of God. We need to understand who Mary is, properly.

First, we have already said in our Creed that we believe that Jesus is both fully Human and Divine and inseparably so. If His Godness is inseparable from His Man-ness, then we can't say that Mary only gave birth to the Man bit of Jesus because that would be separating the inseparable. If Mary is Jesus' mother, and Jesus is God, then it follows that Mary is indeed the Mother of God. We have seen that argument already and it is worth repeating so that we do understand what it means.

We can go further. If Jesus is the King of Heaven, and Mary is Jesus' mother, then Mary is the Queen Mother of Heaven. There's nothing complicated here. We have shown that Mary is the Queen of Heaven, not as the wife of a king but as the mother of a king. In the second chapter of the first book of Kings, we read:

> And Adonijah the son of Haggith came to Bathsheba the mother of Solomon. And she said, Comest thou peaceably? And he said, Peaceably. He said moreover, I have somewhat to say unto thee. And she said, Say on. And he said, Thou knowest that the kingdom was mine, and that all Israel set their faces on me, that I should reign: howbeit the kingdom is turned about, and is become my brother's: for it was his from the LORD. And now I ask one petition of thee, deny me not. And she said unto him, Say on. And he said, Speak, I pray thee, unto Solomon the king, (for he will not say thee nay,) that he give me Abishag the Shunammite to wife. And Bathsheba said, Well; I will speak for thee unto the king. Bathsheba therefore went unto king Solomon, to speak unto him for Adonijah. And the king rose up to meet her, and bowed himself unto her, and sat down on

> his throne, and caused a seat to be set for the king's mother; and she sat on his right hand. Then she said, I desire one small petition of thee; I pray thee, say me not nay. And the king said unto her, Ask on, my mother: for I will not say thee nay.[130]

This puts her in a unique position with regard to humanity. She is always where her son is. We have seen that asking the saints to pray for us is a reasonable thing. We can ask Mary to pray for us too, and we can cultivate her support. If we are in the same community as her, then we must be in the same community as her son. Although Adonijah was asking for something reprehensible, King Solomon still honoured his mother and listened to her. How much more will Jesus who is better than Solomon honour and listen to His mother?

The Early Church believes that Mary was sinless, i.e. that she did nothing wrong in her life.[131] The Early Church also believes that after she died, she rose and was taken up to God like Enoch and Elijah. There is no hard evidence for this in the Bible, but we should take care to listen to the Fathers of the Church who were writing as the Bible was being put together. Even if we believe, like St Thomas Aquinas, that Mary was not free from sin, it still does not stop her from being the Queen of Heaven.

Since she is the Queen of Heaven, Mary deserves much respect and veneration, more than any other saint. Through her the Incarnation took place. It was her "yes" to God that allowed Jesus to be born, live, die, and live again for us. Remember, God always give us the choice to obey Him or not. Mary chose to do so at great

---

[130] I Kings ii.13.20
[131] St Matthew xii.31

personal cost to her, and the results are wonderful! She has to receive our love for that.

However, Mary is not to be worshipped. She would hate that! She always points to her son Who gave Himself as the sacrifice for our sins, and Who saves us from Hell. She is a creature just like we are, and this gives us the right to approach her, and we should not be afraid of asking for her prayers.

Exercise 7.3
If you have never asked Mary to pray for you before, pray the Hail Mary or Salve Regina from the Appendix. If it troubles you, then ask the Holy Ghost to show you why and discuss it with your Mentor.

Angels and Archangels
The word "angel" simply means "messenger," so in some sense anyone who carries a message is an angel. That will be good news for postmen! However, by angel, we usually mean the spiritual beings who minister to God beyond the world that we can see. In fact, properly speaking, they are spirits whose job is to be angels. We say that we believe in God the maker of all things visible and invisible. The angels form part of the invisible world and usually remain invisible.

A Christian should believe in angels, for it is by the Archangel Gabriel that Mary was told that she would be the Mother of God.[132] Isaiah saw the Seraphim around the throne of God.[133] Ezekiel had a very strange encounter with a chariot which seemed to be made out of an angelic being.[134] There are angels galore in the Book of Revelation. It's important to know that these beings

---

[132] St Luke i.26-38
[133] Isaiah vi
[134] Ezekiel i

exist because they do influence the world but the popular picture of human beings becoming angels after they die is not true. Apart from the Cherubim and Seraphim, the Bible doesn't even say if angels have wings!

Jesus says, "Take heed that ye despise not one of these little ones; for I say unto you, That in heaven their angels do always behold the face of my Father which is in heaven."[135] This would suggest that human beings have some association with angels, and leads us to believe that we may have guardian angels. An angel rescues St Peter from prison,[136] and the great warrior Archangel St Michael fights against the Devil for us in Heaven.[137]

If we do have guardian angels, then it is not usually their job to converse with us, but rather to assist us invisibly. We certainly should not be focussing on them as some people do as, like the saints, the job of the angels is to bring us closer to God. Our focus must be on Him and Him alone. There is nothing wrong, however with seeking the help of the angels when we are feeling embattled by sin and temptation. A good prayer is the St Michael prayer in the Appendix.

Exercise 7.4
Read the St Michael prayer through. Does St Michael have the power to defeat Satan?

The Devil
In Baptism, we are to fight against sin, the World and the Devil. Many people think these days that the existence of the Devil is absurd yet they miss something quite important if they do!

---
[135] St Matthew xviii.10
[136] Acts xii
[137] Revelation xii

Throughout the Bible, there stalks a figure who is intent on destroying God's creation. We see him as the serpent in Genesis and as the dragon in the Book of Revelation. We see him tempting Jesus in the wilderness and we see him taunt God in the Book of Job.[138]

Isaiah says,

> How art thou fallen from heaven, O Lucifer, son of the morning! how art thou cut down to the ground, which didst weaken the nations! For thou hast said in thine heart, I will ascend into heaven, I will exalt my throne above the stars of God: I will sit also upon the mount of the congregation, in the sides of the north: I will ascend above the heights of the clouds; I will be like the most High. Yet thou shalt be brought down to hell, to the sides of the pit.[139]

This has led many to believe that the Devil, or Satan, or Lucifer, is an Archangel of God who has rebelled against Him and will spend Eternity apart from Him in Hell. Indeed, by rebelling in this way, it may be that it is the Devil who created Hell by seeking separation from God.

When the Pharisees seek to denounce Jesus, He replies, "Ye are of your father the devil, and the lusts of your father ye will do. He was a murderer from the beginning, and abode not in the truth, because there is no truth in him. When he speaketh a lie, he speaketh of his own: for he is a liar, and the father of it."[140] Thus the Devil is known as the Father of Lies.

It is said that, if you want to get away with a lie, you must wrap it up in the truth. You have already seen that when we looked at

---

[138] Job i-ii
[139] Isaiah xiv.14-15
[140] St John viii.44

"Lead us not into Temptation." The Devil twists God's word so that it sounds appealing to do the wrong thing.

One of the biggest lies that the Devil tells is that he does not exist, and thus we come to believe that Evil isn't as bad as it seems. Or he tries to persuade us that he is ridiculous and thus that the idea of angels, saints and even God Himself are ridiculous too. Many films like to explore the idea of Evil and sensationalise it so that it ceases to become believable.

Another powerful lie that the Devil tells is that he is equal in power to God, that he is another god himself. He is not. He is another creation of God who has used his free-will to abandon God and seeks to tear down mankind with him. Christians need to be concerned about his activity by looking out for evil. We should resist it as far as we can, but we must be aware that we need God to help us overcome evil properly.

St Peter says, "Be sober, be vigilant; because your adversary the devil, as a roaring lion, walketh about, seeking whom he may devour: Whom resist stedfast in the faith, knowing that the same afflictions are accomplished in your brethren that are in the world."[141] St James says, "Submit yourselves therefore to God. Resist the devil, and he will flee from you."[142]

The Devil can be resisted, so take heart and trust God!

Exercise 7.5

What frightens you most about the Devil? How can you see that it is a lie?

---

[141] I Peter v.8-9
[142] James iv.7

Miracles

In an age of Science, miracles seem to be absurd. We don't hear of the miracle healings that took place in Jesus' time. A miracle is a sign which God performs that appear out of the ordinary, and appear to subvert what we understand in our science. While He was on earth with us, Jesus uses miracles to demonstrate that He is exactly who He says He is. Even His saints and apostles have been able to perform miracles in His name. Are these merely just myths?

The trouble is that we think that, because they would break the laws of nature, miracles are impossible or that we would be silly to believe that one occurred. The trouble is that, if this were true, then we would never be able to have enough evidence to say that a miracle occurred. This also undermines the way we do science!

It is also interesting to notice the miracles that Jesus does do and the ones He refuses to do. He will turn water into wine,[143] make blind eyes see,[144] restore withered hands,[145] the deaf hear,[146] the lame walk,[147] and raise the dead,[148] walk on water.[149] There's nothing that He does that actually breaks the laws of nature. One may wonder, of course, how he feeds five thousand people with so little, but He does honour what is created. If we look at what He does not do, we see it is because it violates the nature and purpose of a miracle.

---

[143] St John ii.1-11
[144] E.g. St Mark viii.22-26
[145] St Mark iii.1-3
[146] St Mark vii.31-37
[147] St Matthew xii.9-13
[148] E.g. St John xi.1-44
[149] St Matthew xiv.22-34

The Devil tempts Jesus to turn stones into bread.[150] Even when He feeds the five thousand[151] and the four thousand,[152] Jesus doesn't turn anything into bread but rather builds on what He has. In turning water into wine, He merely adds what is necessary to water which makes it wine. He doesn't corrupt nature. Nor does He use it to show off, like throwing Himself off of the temple and being caught by angels. God doesn't need to show off!

Miracles are not for showing off, and they do not go against what has been created. If they are not for showing off, then it doesn't matter whether we believe that a particular miracle has occurred or not. Christians have to believe that miracles can happen because we trust Jesus, we don't need to believe that everything that presents itself as a miracle really is one.

Most of the time, miracles occur today, but aren't reported by the mainstream press except to make Christians look silly. That's okay – we are to become fools for Christ. However, Christians can look out and see God's miracles around them. They are there to bring joy and wonder back into our lives. Jesus says that we should always seek the kingdom of God like a little child,[153] i.e. with a capacity for awe and wonder.

Exercise 7.6

Have you ever experienced something miraculous? If you have think about what made it miraculous. If not, then pray that your eyes may be opened to the work that God is still doing in the world today.

---

[150] St Matthew iv.3
[151] St Matthew xiv.13-21
[152] St Matthew xv.32-xvi.10
[153] St Matthew xviii.4

Prayer books, Breviaries and Missals

As we have said, the Anglican Catholic Church shares much of its History with the Church of England. This includes the history of the Reformation. At the Reformation, the liturgy was translated into English by Archbishop Thomas Cranmer and Bishop Miles Coverdale and compiled into the Book of Common Prayer which is held in a place of honour by most Anglicans. The Book of Common Prayer went through several revisions, many of which were to reflect the adoption of more Protestant attitudes and ideas. While the Anglican Catholic Church relies on the Primitive Church to work out what the Church teaches, it still relies on the Book of Common Prayer for the way we pray, i.e. our liturgy.

These days, the Anglican Catholic Church uses only liturgical texts which go along with the first Book of Common Prayer which was written in 1549. We have Missals (books for the Mass) and Breviaries (books for praying the Daily Prayers) which are based on the Prayer Book, but which emphasise the Catholic nature of that Prayer Book.

We still use the old language for much the same reason that we still see Shakespeare plays in the Elizabethan language. In so doing, we are saying our prayers in a very precise version of English that we can understand (with some work occasionally) but which other members of the Church have said since the Sixteenth Century. This is also why we have taken our Bible quotations from the Authorised Version (the King James Version) because it supports our belief that the way we pray is the way we believe. It is hard to get into at first, but once you get used to it, you can find yourself standing beside so many Christians saying the same thing the world over. In that sense, this old language has taken over from Latin which the Roman Catholic Church stopped using exclusively in the 1960s.

When you go to public worship in the Anglican Catholic Church, you will therefore find us using the Liturgy in English but which is a translation of a much older liturgy. It will be a bit difficult to get into first, but perseverance is the key. As the Anglican Catholic Church grows, we may be able to use music associated with these texts which does justice to their beauty. If you do get lost, or confused, just listen and watch and ask God to let you hear His voice. Above all, it is important to learn to pray what you are reading.

Exercise 7.7
Ask your priest what books he uses for the liturgy. See if you can find a copy to read through and study at your leisure.

The Blessed Sacrament

We have seen in the Mass that Anglican Catholics believe in the Real Presence of Jesus in the consecrated host which we call the Blessed Sacrament. This means that there are some important conclusions to draw. If your church has a tabernacle in it (a cupboard on the altar containing the Blessed Sacrament) then you must remember that Jesus, the King of Kings, Our Lord and God is really there, really present for you to encounter.

Exercise 7.8
How would you react if you saw Jesus standing beside you?

It is proper, then, to genuflect (kneel on your right knee) before the tabernacle in recognition of Jesus being there. All our actions in church must respect the fact that Jesus is there. Watch the priest as he moves about. How he bows and genuflects at solemn moments.

It is important to remember that we are not bowing to a bit of bread. As we have seen Jesus has promised us His flesh to eat, and He is faithful to us. We must remember this carefully.

Some parishes will hold a service called Benediction. During this service, the Blessed Sacrament is placed in a sun-like container called a monstrance. The priest will pick up the monstrance and bless us with it extending Jesus' blessing to us straight from His very presence. This is not an obligatory service, so if you're not comfortable with it, you need not attend.

Ikons and Idols

In an Anglican Catholic Church, you will often see statues, pictures and ikons. In ikon is a particular style of picture which is "written" (i.e. painted under strict conditions) on wood. It is the custom to bow towards statues and ikons, in order to venerate the person they depict.

Exercise 7.9

Find a photograph of someone you love. How do you feel when you look at it?

In the past, some people have objected violently against ikons and statues claiming that they are idols, the graven images forbidden in the Ten Commandments. However, the Early Church settled this question in the eighth century when it pointed out that, as a human being, Jesus has an image. When we see that image, it is natural to have feelings of worship, not of the image, but the person it depicts. Just like a photograph, an ikon brings to mind the person whose picture is drawn there. If it is a picture of a saint, then we venerate the saint and think about what they did in their life and the way that their merits affect us now. If it is an ikon of Our Lady Mary, then we venerate it and remember her status as Queen of Heaven and act accordingly. If it is an ikon of the Lord Jesus then we are seeing a picture of God. We are not worshipping stone, paint and wood: we worship the God who is depicted.

This is why crucifixes are also acceptable in the Anglican Catholic Church. They serve as a reminder that Christ's death achieves something on our behalf. It is the custom to kiss a crucifix when we see it in honour of the love that it shows.

An idol, on the other hand, is anything that we worship INSTEAD of God. This is why we have to be careful in our attitude to ikons as we do not want them to become graven images and thus idols. We must always focus on the person depicted.

The Church Year and its Seasons

The Church has a cycle of feasts and seasons that it celebrates yearly. Some you may know well, such as Christmas and Easter, others you may not know so well such as Rogationtide and Corpus Christi.

The Church Year is comprised of fixed feasts and moveable feasts. This comes about because the feast of Easter is determined by the lunar calendar (determined by the Moon and thus moveable) and Christmas is determined by the solar calendar (determined by the Sun and thus fixed). This makes for some interesting liturgical variations from year to year. In the Church, a liturgical day starts at sunset of the calendar day before. This means, for example, that, liturgically speaking, Christmas day begins at sunset on the 24th December. Each season has a liturgical colour in which all the material on the altar and elsewhere have the same colour.

The Church Year runs as follows.

Advent

Advent Sunday is the fourth Sunday before Christmas and is the first day of the liturgical year. Advent is the season of penitence and anticipation waiting for the coming of Christ. It has the colour purple in honour of the penitential nature, except for the third Sunday in Advent which has the colour rose.

Christmastide

Christmastide begins on Christmas day and properly lasts until Candlemas on February 2nd. Until after the first Sunday after Epiphany, the liturgical colour is white or gold. It is a time of celebration!

Epiphanytide

Epiphanytide begins with the feast of the Epiphany (revelation of Jesus as God) at sunset on the 5th January and lasts until Septuagesima which is the third Sunday before Lent. From the second Sunday after Epiphany onwards, the liturgical colour is green.

Gesimatide

The three Sundays before Lent are Septuagesima, Sexagesima and Quinquagesima which represent seventy, sixty and fifty days before Easter. This is a time also known as Great Lent in which we begin to prepare ourselves for the fasting and abstinence of Lent. The liturgical colour is purple.

Lent

Lent begins on Ash Wednesday, the Wednesday after Quinquagesima, and lasts until Easter Day. There are forty days of fasting and abstinence in Lent plus six Sundays which are traditionally non-fast days. The liturgical colour remains purple apart from the fourth Sunday in Lent which is Rose.

Passiontide

Passion Sunday is the Fifth Sunday in Lent and begins the last two weeks before Easter. From this point on, all the statues, pictures, crucifixes, and ikons in church are veiled to remind us that before His crucifixion, Jesus hid Himself from the people.

Holy Week

Holy Week begins on Palm Sunday, the Sunday before Easter which celebrates Jesus' entry into Jerusalem on the back of a donkey. Holy Week ends with the Holy Triduum.

The Holy Triduum

Triduum means three days. From the Evening of Maundy Thursday (the Thursday in Holy Week) to the Evening of Easter Day are three liturgical days – Good Friday (the day of crucifixion), Holy Saturday (the day on which Jesus rests in the tomb) and Easter Day (the day of Resurrection). It is worth noting that the names of festivals such as Christmas, specifically include an explicit Judeo-Christian reference. If Easter were to follow that principle, it might be named after the Passover (Pesach in Hebrew), or its correlative word Pasch(al). However, Easter derives from the pagan name 'Eostre' so perhaps we should return to the Old English way of calling Easter, Pasch.[154] On Maundy Thursday, the sanctuary is stripped of colour and left bare to represent Jesus emptying Himself of His divinity. Good Friday has the colour black. On Easter Day, the sanctuary is refurnished with white or gold.

Eastertide (or Paschaltide)

We celebrate Eastertide for six weeks. On the Thursday after the fifth Sunday after Easter, we celebrate the Feast of Jesus'

---

[154] With thanks to Fr Miles Maylor.

ascension into Heaven. The liturgical colour remains white or gold.

Whitsun (or Pentecost)

When Eastertide has finished, we celebrate the descent of the Holy Ghost at Pentecost. This is also called Whitsun (White Sunday) as many people are baptised or confirmed on this day and would naturally be wearing white. Ironically, the liturgical colour is red, a colour used when we say masses on the feasts of apostles and martyrs.

Trinitytide

The Sunday after Whitsun is Trinity Sunday when we celebrate God as Holy Trinity. The Thursday after Trinity Sunday is the feast of Corpus Christi in which we give thanks for God's gift of the Mass. From then on until Advent, the Sundays in Trinitytide are all green except when they occur as a major saint's day. The last Sunday in October is the celebration of Christ the King.

There are other important days in the Church Calendar, saint's days and Ember days, and Rogation days, but these are worth you finding out for yourself! There are also days when it is of great importance for you to attend Church, especially for Mass. These are called Holy Days of Obligation, though remember that the worship of God should come from the heart, not from a list of things to do.

Specifically, you should go to church:

- On all Sundays of the Year;
- On Christmas Day ;
- Over the Triduum and especially on Easter Day;
- On the feast of the Epiphany (6th January);
- On the feast of the Annunciation (25th March);

- On the feast of the Ascension;
- On All Saints' Day (1st November);
- On the feast of Corpus Christi;
- On the feast of the Transfiguration (6th August);

You should observe a fast on

- The forty days of Lent (the Sundays in Lent are NOT fast days);
- Almost all Fridays in the year;
- The Ember Days.

Exercise 7.10

As your priest if you might look at his Ordo – his calendar of feasts for the year. Identify the seasons that we have mentioned, and see if you can adapt your prayer life to the seasons.

Chapter 8: Who am I?

You have now seen a very brief guide to the basics of the Christian Faith as we Anglican Catholics understand it. There is so much more to explore and by now you will probably have a lot of questions and a lot of things that you want to explore yourself. This is fine! Now's the time to reflect and take stock of who you are and how your faith is developing.

Your Prayer Life
1) Do you pray daily?
2) Do you have a set time or pattern for prayer?
3) Do you pray regularly with others?
4) Do you pray from a book?
5) Do you have silent prayer?
6) How does your prayer life fit in the Church?
7) Do you pray the Lord's Prayer daily?
8) Do you pray the Apostle's Creed very often?
9) Do you pray any other prayers daily?
10) If you pray from a book, do you pay attention to the words you are praying?

Your Study
1) Do you read the Bible daily?
2) Do you have a set time of day for reading the Bible?
3) Do you have a lectionary to follow?
4) Do you read the Bible with a commentary?
5) Do you read the Bible with others?
6) Do you read anything from the Church Fathers?
7) What do you do when you don't really understand a passage?
8) What do you do if the Bible passage challenges your belief?

9) Do you study the Creed?
10) Do you listen carefully to the sermon at Mass?

Your Work as a Christian

1) Do you pray before you work to give that work to God?
2) Do you recall the works of mercy often?
3) Do you go to Church often?
4) Do you fast?
5) Do you give alms?
6) Do you think about how you will love God each day?
7) Do you think about how you will love your neighbour each day?
8) Do you look for opportunities to serve God in your everyday work?
9) Do you examine your life for sin?
10) Do you pray before you sleep?

Your Relationship with God

1) How do you know that you love God?
2) How do you know that you love your neighbour?
3) Do you confess your sins to God regularly? In the sacrament of Confession?
4) How do know you are repenting of your sins?
5) Do you thank God for His goodness?
6) Do you seek first the kingdom of God and His Righteousness on a daily basis?
7) Do you recognise Jesus in the Blessed Sacrament?
8) Do you venerate crucifixes and ikons of Jesus?
9) Do you ask for the presence of the Holy Ghost?
10) Do you want to be transformed by God into the human being He wants you to be?

Chapter 9: What is going to happen to me?

It is now time to look at how you are going to become a member of the Church. You may be about to be Baptised, Confirmed, or Received. How will that take place? What will you have to do? And what will be done to you?

Reception

The simplest service is Reception into the Anglican Catholic Church. It is not a sacrament, but essentially in saying that you want to be received, you say that you recognise the Anglican Catholic Church to be your spiritual home and that you wish to abide by its practices and follow its leadership. In fact that's pretty much all the service is. You effectively state the above and promise to follow the spiritual leadership of the Bishop of your Diocese in all things lawful and honest.

You are being received because you have already been validly Baptised and Confirmed and therefore already a full member of the Church. After you have stated your intention, you will then be received formally by your priest or by the Bishop of the Diocese should he wish to receive you himself. While the Bishop is the one to whom you will have expressed your desire to be received, it is often the case in the Anglican Catholic Church that the Bishop will delegate your parish priest to receive you on his behalf.

Baptism

There are a couple of Baptismal rites that may be used. The rite in the Book of Common Prayer is simpler than that of the Western Rite. The Western Rite contains exorcisms which sound rather alarming. There is nothing to be worried about though. An exorcism sends away any evil spirits that are lurking around to prevent you from being Baptised and thus inoculated against sin.

An exorcism states that you are a beloved child of God and that Evil has no business in your life.

Both rites contain declarations and promises that you will have to make as your commitment to the Church. You will be asked if you renounce evil, if you repent of your sins, and if you turn to Christ. You will be asked to declare your faith in God, Father, Son and Holy Ghost. The priest will then pour water on you (or even dip you in water if there is a font big enough) and Baptise you in the name of the same Holy Trinity that you've just put your faith in. From this point on, you will receive the full grace of the sacrament, and be a full member of the Church. You may receive a white garment (a symbol of your wedding garment that all Christians are given in the Book of Revelation) you also may receive a candle (a symbol of the light of Christ that all Christians must bear).

Confirmation

Again, there are a couple of rites that may be used at your Confirmation. If you haven't been Baptised at the same service, then you will be asked, like at Baptism, that you renounce evil, repent of sins and turn to Christ. You will be asked to declare your faith in the Holy Trinity.

The Bishop will then place his hands upon your head and say, "receive the Holy Ghost." From this moment on you will receive the full grace of the sacrament. After this, the bishop may tap you (gently!) on the cheek to remind you that you will have to suffer for Christ.

And now?

And now, we rejoice at having you as part of the Church. Wherever you are and wherever we are, we rejoice in your membership and having you work with us to bring God's love and blessing to the world. Always remember, no matter in whatever circumstance you find yourself, that the Church stands with you and for you, that you are loved fully, completely, and uncompromisingly by God and by every Christian who practises what they preach.

St Paul says, "...I am persuaded, that neither death, nor life, nor angels, nor principalities, nor powers, nor things present, nor things to come, Nor height, nor depth, nor any other creature, shall be able to separate us from the love of God, which is in Christ Jesus our Lord."[155]

God bless you richly and may you find His joy in your life's work.

You can keep in touch with news of the Anglican Catholic Church in the United Kingdom on our Website:

www.anglicancatholic.org.uk

and around the world:

www.anglicancatholic.org

---

[155] Romans viii.38-39

Appendix
Selected Prayers to Learn and Use
Sign of the Cross
In the name of the Father, and of the Son, and of the Holy Ghost. Amen.

Making the Sign of the Cross works as follows:

In the name of the Father [touch your forehead with the fingertips of your right hand], and of the Son [touch your tummy], and of the Holy [left shoulder] Ghost [right shoulder]. Amen.

The Lord's Prayer
Our Father, who art in heaven, hallowed be thy name; thy kingdom come, thy will be done, on earth as it is in heaven. Give us this day our daily bread and forgive us our trespasses, as we forgive those who trespass against us and lead us not into temptation, but deliver us from evil. Amen.

Hail Mary
Hail Mary, full of grace, the Lord is with thee. Blessed art thou among women and blessed is the fruit of thy womb, Jesus. Holy Mary, mother of God, pray for us sinners now and at the hour of our death. Amen.

Glory Be
Glory be to the Father, and to the Son, and to the Holy Ghost, as it was in the beginning, is now, and ever shall be, world without end. Amen.

Apostles' Creed
I believe in God, the Father almighty, Maker of heaven and earth: And in Jesus Christ, His only Son, our Lord: Who was conceived by the Holy Ghost, born of the Virgin Mary: suffered under Pontius Pilate, Was crucified, dead and buried: He descended into hell; the third day He rose again from the dead: He ascended into heaven And sitteth on the right hand of God the Father Almighty: From thence He shall come to judge the quick and the dead. I believe in the Holy Ghost, the holy Catholic Church; the Communion of Saints; The Forgiveness of sins: the Resurrection of the body: and the Life everlasting. Amen.

Come, Holy Ghost
Come, Holy Ghost, fill the hearts of Thy faithful and enkindle in them the fire of Thy love. Send forth Thy Spirit, and they shall be created. And Thou shalt renew the face of the earth.

Grace before meals
Bless us, O Lord, and these Thy gifts, which we are about to receive from Thy bounty. Through Christ our Lord. Amen.

Salve Regina
Hail, Holy Queen, Mother of mercy, our life, our sweetness, and our hope. To thee do we cry, poor banished children of Eve. To thee do we send up our sighs, mourning and weeping in this vale of tears. Turn then, most gracious advocate, thine eyes of mercy towards us and after this, our exile, show unto us the blessed fruit of thy womb, Jesus. O clement, O loving, O sweet Virgin Mary.

Prayer to St Michael the Archangel
St. Michael the Archangel, defend us in battle; be our defence against the wickedness and snares of the devil. May God rebuke him, we humbly pray, and do thou, O prince of the heavenly host, by the power of God, thrust into hell Satan and all the other evil

spirits who prowl about the world seeking the ruin of souls. Amen.

The Athanasian Creed

WHOSOEVER will be saved: before all things it is necessary that he hold the Catholick Faith. Which Faith except every one do keep whole and undefiled: without doubt he shall perish everlastingly.

And the Catholick Faith is this: That we worship one God in Trinity, and Trinity in Unity; Neither confounding the Persons: nor dividing the Substance. For there is one Person of the Father, another of the Son: and another of the Holy Ghost. But the Godhead of the Father, of the Son, and of the Holy Ghost, is all one: the Glory equal, the Majesty co-eternal. Such as the Father is, such is the Son: and such is the Holy Ghost. The Father uncreate, the Son uncreate: and the Holy Ghost uncreate. The Father incomprehensible, the Son incomprehensible: and the Holy Ghost incomprehensible. The Father eternal, the Son eternal: and the Holy Ghost eternal. And yet they are not three eternals: but one eternal.

As also there are not three incomprehensibles, nor three uncreated: but one uncreated, and one incomprehensible. So likewise the Father is Almighty, the Son Almighty: and the Holy Ghost Almighty. And yet they are not three Almighties: but one Almighty. So the Father is God, the Son is God: and the Holy Ghost is God. And yet they are not three Gods: but one God. So likewise the Father is Lord, the Son Lord: and the Holy Ghost Lord. And yet not three Lords: but one Lord.

For like as we are compelled by the Christian verity: to acknowledge every Person by himself to be God and Lord; So are we forbidden by the Catholick Religion: to say there be three

Gods, or three Lords. The Father is made of none: neither created, nor begotten. The Son is of the Father alone: not made, nor created, but begotten. The Holy Ghost is of the Father and of the Son: neither made, nor created, nor begotten, but proceeding. So there is one Father, not three Fathers; one Son, not three Sons: one Holy Ghost, not three Holy Ghosts.

And in this Trinity none is afore, or after other: none is greater, or less than another; But the whole three Persons are co-eternal together: and co-equal. So that in all things, as is aforesaid: the Unity in Trinity, and the Trinity in Unity is to be worshipped. He therefore that will be saved: must thus think of the Trinity.

Furthermore it is necessary to everlasting salvation: that he also believe rightly the Incarnation of our Lord Jesus Christ. For the right Faith is that we believe and confess: that our Lord Jesus Christ, the Son of God, is God and Man; God, of the Substance of the Father, begotten before the worlds: and Man, of the Substance of his Mother, born in the world; Perfect God, and Perfect Man: of a reasonable soul and human flesh subsisting; Equal to the Father, as touching his Godhead: and inferior to the Father, as touching his Manhood. Who although he be God and Man: yet he is not two, but one Christ; One, not by conversion of the Godhead into flesh: but by taking of the Manhood into God; One altogether, not by confusion of Substance: but by unity of Person. For as the reasonable soul and flesh is one man: so God and Man is one Christ. Who suffered for our salvation: descended into hell, rose again the third day from the dead. He ascended into heaven, he sitteth on the right hand of the Father, God Almighty: from whence he shall come to judge the quick and the dead. At whose coming all men shall rise again with their bodies: and shall give account for their own works. And they that have done good shall go into life everlasting: and they that have done evil into everlasting fire. This is the Catholick Faith: which except a man believe faithfully, he cannot be saved.

Glory be to the Father, and to the Son: and to the Holy Ghost; As it was in the beginning, is now, and ever shall be: world without end. Amen.

The Works of Mercy

The Seven Corporal Works of Mercy
1) Feed the hungry.
2) Give water to the thirsty.
3) Clothe the naked.
4) Shelter the homeless.
5) Visit the sick.
6) Visit the imprisoned, or ransom the captive.
7) Bury the dead.

The Seven Spiritual Works of Mercy
1) Instruct the ignorant.
2) Counsel the doubtful.
3) Admonish sinners (i.e. warn them wisely).
4) Bear patiently those who wrong us.
5) Forgive offences.
6) Console the afflicted.
7) Pray for the living and the dead.

Index

absolution, 95, 102
abstinence, 48, 49, 78, 127
adultery, 50, 80, 83, 103
Almighty, 14, 16, 17, 18, 21, 71, 138
almsgiving, 49
Anglican Catholic, 10, 11, 12, 27, 31, 48, 56, 59, 97, 102, 103, 123, 124, 125, 126, 133
Apostles, 15, 40, 73, 105, 107, 137
Apostles' Creed, 15, 73, 137
Appollinarians, 22
Ascension, 27, 130
Athanasian Creed, 15, 138
Baptised. *See* Baptism
Baptism, 10, 33, 41, 43, 53, 59, 78, 94, 95, 99, 100, 118, 133, 134
Benediction, 125
Bible, 18, 20, 29, 55, 56, 116, 118, 119, 123, 131
Bishop, 64, 105, 106, 107, 123, 133, 134
blessing, 49, 61, 85, 93, 96, 125, 135
Book of Common Prayer, 123, 133
Church of England, 12, 34, 123
clergy, 105, 108
communion, 34, 74, 75, 96, 137
Confession, 100, 101, 102, 132
Confirmation, 33, 78, 99, 100, 134

Corpus Christi, 126, 129, 130
creation, 72, 90, 119, 120
deacon, 105, 108, 109
Death, 24, 43, 103, 111, 113
Devil, 71, 86, 118, 119, 120, 122
Docetists, 22, 34
Easter, 25, 26, 27, 126, 127, 128, 129
Eternity, 30, 70, 73, 74, 112, 119
Eucharist, 96, 98
Evensong, 15, 60
fasting, 25, 48, 49, 78, 127
Father, 14, 16, 17, 19, 20, 22, 25, 27, 28, 29, 30, 31, 32, 34, 53, 62, 63, 68, 70, 91, 94, 95, 102, 118, 119, 134, 136, 137, 138
forgiveness, 69, 71, 95, 97, 98, 101, 137
good deeds, 57, 85
Grace, 78, 93, 137
heaven, 14, 17, 18, 21, 22, 25, 26, 27, 28, 50, 53, 62, 63, 69, 80, 95, 118, 119, 136, 137, 139
Hell, 112, 113, 114, 117, 119
Holy Ghost, 14, 21, 27, 28, 29, 30, 31, 32, 33, 41, 95, 99, 100, 101, 102, 103, 105, 106, 107, 117, 129, 132, 134, 136, 138
Holy Spirit. *See* Holy Ghost
ikon, 125
judgement, 112
Kingdom, 12, 28, 65, 66

Law, 42
lectionary, 131
liturgical colour, 126, 127, 129
liturgy, 33, 59, 65, 97, 123, 124
marriage, 15, 83, 102, 103
Mary, 14, 21, 22, 115, 116, 117, 125, 136, 137
Mass, 14, 24, 27, 36, 59, 60, 68, 96, 97, 98, 109, 123, 124, 129, 132
Mattins, 15, 60
merits, 75, 85, 125
miracle, 102, 121, 122
moral compass, 53, 55
Mystery, 93
New Testament, 40, 68
Nicene Creed, 14, 15, 31, 45, 94
Old Testament, 16, 24, 32, 40, 97
penitence, 48, 127
prayer, 19, 21, 30, 33, 48, 49, 59, 62, 64, 72, 84, 104, 107, 118, 130, 131
priest, 10, 16, 17, 19, 48, 49, 60, 64, 65, 95, 98, 101, 102, 103, 105, 108, 109, 124, 125, 130, 133, 134
reconciliation, 69, 98
Repentance, 52
Resurrection, 26, 43, 45, 73, 112, 128
Roman Catholic, 11, 34, 38, 123

sacrament, 40, 93, 94, 96, 98, 99, 102, 105, 132, 133, 134
sacrifice, 23, 24, 36, 85, 88, 97, 98, 117
saints, 37, 40, 54, 68, 73, 74, 75, 87, 116, 118, 120, 121, 137
salvation, 14, 21, 25, 38, 45, 59, 71, 139
Science, 19, 121
sin, 21, 24, 25, 36, 41, 42, 43, 44, 53, 54, 55, 69, 70, 71, 77, 79, 83, 85, 88, 89, 91, 95, 100, 101, 112, 113, 116, 118, 132, 133
Son, 14, 19, 20, 21, 23, 27, 29, 30, 31, 32, 81, 95, 102, 134, 136, 137, 138
Son of God, 14, 19, 20, 21, 30, 139
St Michael, 118, 137
temptation, 71, 118, 136
Ten Commandments, 50, 51, 89, 125
theological truth, 18
transformation, 114
Trinity, 15, 20, 21, 32, 129, 134, 138
Two Commandments, 51, 58
Works of Mercy, 58, 140
worship, 21, 33, 44, 47, 49, 56, 75, 77, 79, 84, 86, 88, 115, 124, 125, 126, 129, 138

Printed in Great Britain
by Amazon